Ltd to 500 cc

75⁰⁰
6K5
8B

OF BOOKMEN & PRINTERS

# Of Bookmen & Printers
## A Gathering of Memories

## By Ward Ritchie

## dawsons

*A Bookman's Los Angeles* was originally given as a talk to the Zamorano Club and later printed by Grant Dahlstrom in 1970. *Jake Zeitlin* appeared in *AB Bookman*, February 1, 1988. *Paul Landacre* was published by the Book Club of California in 1982. *Merle Armitage, Robinson Jeffers, Jane Grabhorn,* and *C.H. St. John Hornby* and *A Requiem for Lawrence Clark Powell* were all printed in small editions by Laguna Verde. *Paris Adventure* is based on a series of talks given at the University of Arizona, which subsequently published it. It was later expanded as *Art Deco* and published by the Book Club of California. Most of these have been somewhat rewritten for this publication.

ISBN 0-87093-275-6

Published by Dawson's Book Shop
535 North Larchmont Boulevard
Los Angeles, California 90004

# CONTENTS

For Ward a Foreword
*By Lawrence Clark Powell*

# FOR WARD A FOREWORD
## BY LAWRENCE CLARK POWELL

SIXTY YEARS AGO three young Californians were the magnet that drew Ward Ritchie to Dijon on occasional weekends from his apprenticeship with Paris printer François-Louis Schmied. These obscure students were Alfred and Mary Frances Kennedy Fisher and Lawrence Clark Powell. The weekend activities of the four were determined by the nature of the old Burgundian ducal city, which had become a provincial town where its dwellers went to bed early.

After a meal at *Chez* Racouchot, one of France's best restaurants, the four stayed up late in the Fishers's apartment, reading aloud from their own work, teaching Fisher how to shoot craps (and also lose his money), and talking about what they would do when they returned to southern California. Ritchie intended to print, Powell hoped to teach and write, while Fisher had several ideas, mostly vague. As for M.F., she went on knitting — no, not tiny garments, rather a sweater against the cold.

Between Fisher, a minister's son, and Ritchie with head full of Ruskinesque dreams (or was it Pater?), they hatched a plan of a commune somewhere south of Tehachapi where the members would do everything for themselves. This harkened back to the Middle Ages and ahead to hippie time. No matter that none had any land or much money.

The first choice for a site was Baja California, so Powell went to his room for a map of the West Coast, among those he had collected for his work on Jeffers. Scammons Lagoon seemed a likely spot if only for its immemorial *Ojo de Liebre* (Spring of the

Hare), which ensured fresh water. Such planning lasted until late, the hour determined by stamina and the wine level. Meanwhile Fisher read on hypnotically from his epic; Powell told tales of jazz bands on land and sea; and Ritchie spun gossamer verses from old loves. M.F. kept on knitting.

The years passed, and like all prodigals they came home. After a stay on the beach at Laguna, the Fishers went their ways, she to Switzerland and he to New England. Ritchie and Powell stayed and are still staying — well, not quite, since Larry carried Fay off to Arizona in 1971, although they return when necessary to look in on old Wardie.

What of the commune that once lit up the skies over the Côte d'Or? It was transformed into something not dreamed of in 1930. Fashioned by a pragmatic dreamer, another kind of commune came into being at 705 1/2 West Sixth Street in downtown L.A., at the Sign of the Grasshopper. There in the crack-in-the-wall bookshop of Jake Zeitlin gathered the artists and writers who had managed to climb aboard the life raft of the W.P.A.

It was they who relit the flame that had guttered out with the death of Lummis in 1928, although not before Jake had grasped the torch from him, as evidenced in his book of poems presented to Lummis: "To C.F.L., far out on a trail I am trying to follow." Wasn't his shop only a stone's throw from El Alisal? There Jake gave material support to such as Paul Landacre and Edward Weston. Merle Armitage rehearsed his role as The Impresario. Ritchie, Marks, and Dahlstrom fashioned printing to Jake's needs. Powell typed and Fay wrapped books. It was truly a commune.

The Ritchie reminiscences gathered happily here recall those wondrous times. An even fuller treatment will appear in the third volume of Kevin Starr's literary history of California, now in press at Oxford. Most of the participants have left this vale of more laughter than tears. Of the few surviving painters and sculptors, I know that sculptor Gordon Newell is still at work in his Carmel studio. As for Fisher, Armitage, Weston, Landacre, McWilliams, Hanna, Marks, Dahlstrom, and Jake, he the first and last of all, they can now be recalled only in memory, and words such as these of Ward's. M.F. lives venerably in the Valley of the Moon where she rules as Queen Merlin. Powell's desert defection is noted above. Ritchie, the lone local survivor and tireless narrator-printer, dwells productively on Laguna Verde.

So here once again, and probably not for the last time, I salute Ward from a lifetime of affection.

*Tucson, Arizona*
*Bajada of the Santa Catalinas*
*Summer 1989*

OF BOOKMEN & PRINTERS

# I

# A BOOKMAN'S LOS ANGELES
## IN THE 1930S

*During the bleak days of the Great Depression in the 1930s, Los Angeles, paradoxically, experienced a cultural renaissance in arts and architecture, in books and printing, which eventually liberated the town from its provincial reputation.*

IN THE 1930s Los Angeles was not exactly a small town, but it had an intimacy which the subsequent years have lost. There was such a concentration of business that one could run into a dozen acquaintances while walking not more than a few blocks. The big red Pacific Electric cars brought shoppers from miles around, and the yellow street cars crisscrossed the city, all leading to the area we called "downtown."

To me the heart was where the bookstores were. Along with a few bars and some mangy upstairs hotels of questionable morality, they lined both sides of West Sixth Street from Grand Avenue nearly to Figueroa. A few shops hung on the fringes, such as Dawson's, a block away at the corner of Wilshire and Grand, and Louis Epstein's bookstore over on Eighth Street. A half a million books or more were to be seen within this area of a few blocks, and booklovers flocked to the lure. There was variety in both books and establishments. For instance, in Ralph Howey's little English nook one could sink into a soft leather chair and

13

chat about books while stroking a binding by Cobden-Sander-son or looking at the pages of an edition printed by Giambattista Bodoni. Each book was in its place, immaculate and carefully chosen. Or up the street a block, one could gingerly slip into David Kohn's Curio Book Shop, where a hundred thousand books were crammed helter-skelter in bins, piled on the floor, stacked in the basement, with only a bare semblance of order. It was a grimy job searching here for a treasure, since more than a decade of dust was mingled with the books; but for the hunter it was a delightful challenge. No one could possibly anticipate what might be discovered in the mélange. Kohn usually stood noncommittally in the doorway, hat pulled down to his ears, seemingly uninterested, while emitting an occasional eructation that echoed down the canyon of Sixth Street and created minor disturbances in the hotel cribs on the upstairs floors.

Mingled with these shops were Bunster Creeley's Abbey Bookshop, Ben Epstein's Argonaut, Borden's, Roger's, Lof-land's, Holmes's huge emporium of books, several incidental shops whose names I have long forgotten, and, of course, Jake Zeitlin's bookshop and gallery.

The *aficionados* of books were regular visitors to most of these shops, but there gradually developed a division of affection which found the serious, older, and Californiana collectors gathering around "Club" Dawson, while the younger writers, artists, and printers loitered at "Club" Zeitlin.

Zeitlin's first shop was on Hope Street across from the Bible Institute, but he soon moved to 705½ West Sixth Street in a little half-store, just big enough for a couple of hundred books and a minimal gallery where he hung the prints and drawings of local artists. It was here I first saw the books of the great printers of the 1920s — Eric Gill, Francis Meynell of the Nonesuch Press, Robert Gibbings of the Golden Cockerel Press, and

Edwin and Robert Grabhorn of San Francisco. Jake gathered around him a stimulating group of artists and writers — Paul Landacre, Will Connell, Merle Armitage, Arthur Millier, Paul Jordan-Smith, Phil Townsend Hanna, W.W. Robinson, and many others including printers Bruce McCallister, Gregg Anderson, Grant Dahlstrom, and Saul Marks. One dropped by Zeitlin's to see the new books from England and to talk to Jake. There was stimulating action there.

But the favorite haunt of the bookmen of Los Angeles was the spot on Grand Avenue at the corner of Wilshire. There they encountered Ernest Dawson, a master merchandiser of books. He regularly juggled them from table to table and from shelf to shelf. As a result, it always appeared that a new library of books had arrived, keeping his customers constantly interested and inveterate repeaters. There were other inducements. "Father" Dawson, as he was known, never wished to have a book in stock too long. If it lingered on the shelves for over six months, he'd itch to get rid of it. Before long he'd slash the price, and if it didn't sell then, he'd cut the price again. This created an incentive to visit Dawson's regularly, since one could never tell when these reductions would take place. Inevitably, this also led to a game of waiting, watching, and returning as often as possible to check on those books which one might want but thought might again be a victim of Father Dawson's price-cutting pencil. This game of wits sometimes paid off, but often a less patient book-watcher spoiled the game by buying the book one was stalking.

Books were comparatively cheap in the 1930s — great bargains by today's standards — but most of us didn't have much money to fritter on them. Dawson provided for the impoverished with a table of bargains at the street entrance. Here for from ten cents to fifty cents were the books from which I built much of my own library. While books provided a part of the excitement of a visit to Dawson's in those days, more came in observing the parade of bookmen who would drop by several times a week.

I remember many of them in hero worship. I was young and in love with books, and these were men of stature in that world. I doubt if Los Angeles will ever again know quite such an assemblage of bookmen. And for them this kingdom of books was concentrated in such a few blocks that there was an almost constant meeting and mingling.

The king of this small empire was Robert Ernest Cowan. Twice a week he left his hideaway at the William Andrews Clark Library to visit his realm. His was a regal image. His hair was white, his beard and mustache a duplicate of that other monarch, George V. He would pay a visit to most of the shops on Sixth Street before making a final and prolonged appearance at Dawson's. He would curiously inspect a few books and then indulge himself for an hour or so by chatting with the attractive and intelligent girls who worked there. Naturally, he was a favorite with them. To hover close by was a rewarding experience. His knowledge and memory of the books of California were implicit. He spoke slowly and precisely. Each of his words, chosen with care, conveyed with unerring picturesque exactness his thoughts.

Dorothy Bevis, later of the University of Washington Library School, introduced me to Cowan in 1928. When I first commenced printing he suggested a poem by George Arnold on which I could try my teeth. The first stanza read:

Here,
 with my beer
I sit,
 While golden moments flit:

Alas!
They pass
Unheeded by:
And, as they fly,
I,
Being dry,
Sit, idly sipping here,
My beer.

The first commercial, or paid, job I ever had as a printer was commissioned by "Sir Robert." Throughout his whole life no one ever spoke to him by his given name. His dignity was such that even to his friends he was Mr. Cowan. However, in his later years he accepted the affectionate and respectful address of "Sir Robert" by the members of the Zamorano Club. It was for this club that he asked me in 1930 to print a booklet entitled *The Booklover's Litany*. With the characteristic consistency that seemed to persist through my printing career, until I was able to afford a competent proofreader, I misspelled a word, and it had to be, of all my possible choices, the very name of the club, Zamorano.

One of the founder members of the Zamorano Club, Will Clary, recalls that when the formation of the club was contemplated and possible members were being considered, the new man at the Clark Library was suggested as one to be approached. He had recently arrived from San Francisco, and in the 1920s the culture of Los Angeles was held in some scorn by many of the more cultured inhabitants of the north. Mr. Cowan had evidently been influenced while living there. When offered membership in the new club, he declined, remarking that there were hardly enough bookmen in Los Angeles to support such an organization and predicting its early demise. A year later he admitted his error and suggested to the president, Arthur Ellis, that he would like to become a member.

In 1941, as I recall, Cowan gave a talk before the members of the Zamorano Club on "Booksellers of Old San Francisco." I asked him if he had a copy of his manuscript since I thought it should be published. His reply was that he'd never written it, but that it was firmly retained in his memory if I'd like to have it. This was true. He could repeat almost verbatim any anecdote, any conversation, any talk that he gave. We sent a stenographer to his house, and over several sessions he dictated his speech. After transcribing it we sent a copy to him for checking. He called me one day in May of 1942 to say that he'd corrected it and would leave it for me to pick up, as he was going to the hospital for surgery. He never returned.

In the foreword to this book, when it was eventually published, Henry R. Wagner wrote about Cowan in his earlier days as a bookseller in San Francisco:

"I had met Mr. Cowan in 1915 at the San Francisco Fair but it was not until I opened an office in that city in 1917 that I began to buy books from him. By that year he had accumulated a large stock in a small house in which he lived on Treat Avenue. It was one of those old California houses consisting of a basement with a flight of steps leading up to the first floor. Mr. Cowan kept his books mostly in the basement as he had to have some place to sleep."

Wagner was a titan among the bookmen of Los Angeles. He had the rotund figure of a Santa Claus and the same rosy and cherubic countenance. While Cowan had compiled *A Bibliography of the History of California*, Wagner had written an equally important bibliography, *The Plains and the Rockies*, along with many others. His theory was that a bibliography enhances the value of any collection of books. During his long life he accumulated many specialized collections, compiled a bibliography of each, and sold at a good profit.

In 1952 we printed a little book of his called *Sixty Years of Book Collecting* in which he told of his introduction to book collecting and of the some twenty major collections he had accumulated and of their disposal to various institutions.

It was somewhat by chance that he began to specialize rather than continuing to buy random books. Working for the Globe Smelting and Refining Company in Denver, he was sent to Mexico to investigate some ore. While there he found them using an ancient method of refining called the "Patio Process," which was unknown in the United States. The Mexican workers seemed to follow no formula — the method had just been passed on from generation to generation. Seeking more information, he found a book describing the process in Mexico City, printed in 1805. He began seeking more books on the subject, and since his job carried him to several countries, he had many opportunities to discover and buy. In Chile in 1898 and 1899 he found a few, and when he went to London as agent for the American Smelting and Refining Company, he was able to investigate the bookstores of that city. He found books on the "Patio Process" printed as far back as 1540. When he turned this library over to Yale University years later, there were about 600 items.

Henry Wagner remained a bachelor into his fifties, enjoying life. For several of these years he was an avid bridge player, playing almost every afternoon and evening with good success. Suddenly his luck changed, as he told me, and he concluded that cards were partial to the young. He decided upon a new life. He quit his job with the Guggenheims, married, and devoted the remainder of his life, almost a half century, to collecting books and writing them.

He used his books, cramming into his memory an accumulation of knowledge on matters that especially interested him. He used this to good advantage, writing more than 170 authoritative books and articles on a variety of subjects, mostly dealing with voyages and history of the west coast of North America.

As with Cowan, Henry Wagner was a man to whom one enjoyed listening. He had an impressive accumulation of lore and historical knowledge, and it was permanently tucked into his memory. His books were dictated from this reservoir with, as far as I know, hardly a change or correction. In reading his biography, *Bullion to Books,* or any other of his writings, one can almost hear him conversing in the study of his San Marino home.

Wagner belied all modern medical theory. He lived to be ninety-five years old. He was so round and well-fed that he could hardly shuffle down Sixth Street to visit the bookstores once a week, but he managed. He never exercised, he loved whiskey and cigars, he fought violently with his French wife, and yet he outlived most of his annuities.

Henry Wagner was of German parentage and had a stubborn disposition. I feel that I must take some credit in prolonging his life. In September 1947 we had a surprise party at the University Club to celebrate his eighty-fifth birthday. For the occasion, I printed a facsimile and a translation, with a foreword by Wagner, of *Al Bello Sesco,* which was the first poem written and printed in the territory of California. It had originally been printed by Agustín V. Zamorano, California's first printer. The copy we used belonged to Thomas Streeter, who kindly allowed us to reproduce it in facsimile.

At that time we had sitting in the center of our living room the Albion hand press that had originally belonged to Arthur Ellis and later to Grant Dahlstrom. For the occasion I handset and almost completed a single copy of this book in facsimile and translation. Since there was some reluctance in postponing Wagner's birthday, I had to bind an incomplete copy for the presentation. It looked fairly good despite the blank pages at the end, which by good fortune were there for everyone present to sign in his honor.

It was a delightful occasion and to the toasts and accolades, Wagner responded in his usual pleasant and provocative manner. He suggested that one of the most needed bibliographical tools for the Western historian was an index to the six volumes of Bancroft's *History of California.* The members of the Zamorano Club accepted the challenge and over the years accumulated a vast file which eventually was published in two volumes by the University of Southern California.

Each year thereafter, we celebrated Wagner's birthday, gathering at his home, and each year he'd ask me if I'd finished printing *Al Bello Sesco.* I could hardly tell him that our children had smashed the type and I hadn't reset it. So almost another decade passed before I completed the little book and took it over to distribute at one of these birthday parties. I almost wish I hadn't, because I feel that stubborn old Henry would have stuck around another dozen years to be sure that I'd finish it.

While Frederick Hodge was not as habitual an attendant of the "Rites of Sixth Street" as many of the others, he was an important part of the group and, as director of the Southwest Museum, was an authority on Southwest Indians. Fred Hodge was a year or so younger than Wagner and was never quite able to catch up. This must have distressed him since it was always Wagner's birthday that was celebrated and never Hodge's. But he was a great sport and enjoyed the festivities, always being one of the gayest of those present. He lived in Pasadena along my route home, and it was often my pleasure to stop on my way for a visit and a chat.

He'd mix a couple of his special old-fashioneds, with an extra one for his young and attractive wife and perhaps one for Carl Dentzel, who also enjoyed these visits. Hodge was the youngest old man I've ever known. In his nineties he was alert, sinewy, and active, though wrinkled as an old Indian. He was not the man to die in bed, and he finally succumbed while climbing a mountain in New Mexico.

Many years ago I was invited to Washington to do some work with the Government Printing Office. With its customary consideration, the United States Government allotted to me a companion to guide me through the maze of red, white, and blue tape. Her name was Ummie. I don't know what prompted her parents to be so perspicacious in naming their child. I can no longer recall her last name; at the time I couldn't believe her first. After we had introduced ourselves and she learned that I was from southern California, she became interested, saying that she thought she had an uncle who lived somewhere out there. She added that he was the black sheep of the family and most intriguing. As a little girl, she had heard members of her family gossip about his drinking, his smoking, and the fact that one day, without adieu, he'd walked out on his wife and disappeared into the West. She asked if I'd ever run into him. His name was Frederick Webb Hodge. A couple of years later when Ummie visited California, I was able to introduce her to her uncle, and they were delighted with one another.

Somewhat of a loner among the habitués of Sixth Street and Dawson's was John I. Perkins. He was a dapper man, probably in his late sixties or early seventies when I first knew him. He looked like a college boy of the early twenties with his narrow-brimmed flat-top hat jauntily perched on the back of his head and, slim as a youth, eagerly bounced around the shops seeking and searching for beautiful books. He specialized in examples of great printing. His collection was left to Scripps College where it has been an inspiration to many generations of Scripps girls. I visited his home only on one occasion and was amazed. It was a cramped journey through his place, only possible for one as slender as he, and as I was then. Even the stairway passage was hazardous, with bookshelves crowding in from each side. His place reminded me of that of the legendary Renaissance Florentine book collector, Antonio Magliabecchi, whose house, as Dibdin described it, had become "a kind of cave made of piles and masses of books, with hardly any room for his cooking or for the wooden cradle lined with pamphlets which he slung between his shelves for a bed."

When Glen Dawson went to Perkins's home after his death to pack the books for delivery to Scripps College, he found that it was not only books that Perkins collected. He kept everything. In one closet were over sixty pairs of old shoes and in another, a fifty-year collection of string. Dawson was delighted in finding rolls of the special string that had come off the packages of books Perkins had bought at his bookshop.

Father Dawson had a long-standing rule that the shop closed at five o'clock, regardless. Only for John I. Perkins was this rule broken. Perkins would putter and snoop beyond closing time, and Dawson would linger on and wait, sometimes for over an hour, before Perkins made his final selection. But it was worth it, since he seldom bought less than $100 worth of books at a time.

Phil Townsend Hanna was another articulate historian–book collector. He, too, was an amazing man with many interests and talents. He edited *Westways* magazine; wrote *Bohemian Life,* a sprightly monthly publication devoted to eating and drinking; and still found time to write a half-dozen books. Phil collected Western Americana and cookbooks. His collection is now in the library at Scripps College.

He was a thin, bowed man, almost bent to a horizontal position as he walked down Sixth Street from lunch at the California
Club to check if there were any new arrivals at the bookstores. At
Manual Arts High School he was known as "Doc Hanna" when
as head waterboy for the football team, he administered to their
thirst and bruises. A couple of years later he suffered a form of
mountain fever which left him deformed for the rest of his life. It
had no apparent effect on his personality. He was the most
immaculately groomed of all the habitués of booksellers' row
and the one with the greatest capacity for enjoying every deli-
cious crumb of life. He was the heart and master of the Wine and
Food Society of Los Angeles from its beginning in the
mid-1930s until his death in 1957. He nurtured and mothered an
appreciation of great wines and food in those days immediately
after Prohibition, when Los Angeles was hardly a gourmet's
paradise. The local restaurants were then flattered to be chosen
by Phil for one of his dinners and would put on a production.
Nowadays, with a plethora of such groups, they could hardly
care.

For a wisp of a man he had the greatest endurance and the
most amazing capacity for drinking that I have ever witnessed,
and I have had many opportunities to observe him. After the
Wine and Food Society dinners, the insatiable Phil would
always grab a few of us to close the bar and listen to his thought-
ful, penetrating observations on the dishes and wines that had
been served. He never seemed to show the slightest effect of
alcohol. I remember one occasion when Phil was to bring Fed-
eral Judge Pierson Hall to a meeting of the Zamorano Club.
Along with Dr. Marcus Crahan, they stopped on their way at the
California Club for a substantial drink, since only sherry and
wine were served at the Zamorano meetings. They were joined
by Otto Christiansen, and somehow one drink led to another

until the Zamorano meeting hour had passed. They repaired to Marcus Crahan's apartment for further indulging.

The next afternoon I unwittingly dropped in at Dr. Crahan's apartment with some proofs for him to check. Here I found the bar still open and the conversation still stimulating and intelligent, having continued from the previous evening with only the interruption of a few hours' sleep. Only Judge Hall had succumbed and crept off. I was happy to be his replacement. Later that evening (and I must admit that I was beginning to be aware of what we had consumed) it was decided that we should go to Perino's restaurant for dinner.

I was watching Phil Hanna, figuring that after twenty-four hours of almost continuous drinking he might finally show some effects from it. But not Hanna. We arrived and, rather than immediately ordering dinner, he asked for a double martini. He had another before we were served, and, of course, we had wine with our food. When we finally parted he still showed no effects, as I staggered out.

Phil Townsend Hanna's contributions to southern California were many. He encouraged both local artists and writers in *Westways* for over twenty-five years. Back during World War I, in 1917–19, he was night editor of the *Los Angeles Times*. It always amused him to tell the story of General Otis who owned the *Times*. Otis never carried a cent with him since he was recognized and his credit was good anywhere. One day he came storming in to borrow a nickel from Phil. We've always suspected that some newsboy refused to trust him for a copy of his own paper.

Some of the most interesting books I ever bought on the bargain counter at Dawson's were from the library of A. Gaylord Beaman, which they sold after his death. He was a man whose catholic tastes encompassed literature and incidental private press products. Gay was a member of the Zamorano Club and the Authors Club of Hollywood. His business was insurance, but his avocation was authors. No author ever came to Los Angeles without being met at the station by Gay Beaman. He'd greet them and dine them and then take them through the routine of Sixth Street's book row before rounding the corner to Dawson's. Many an author I met there, brought by Gay Beaman — Sherwood Anderson, Rockwell Kent, Christopher Morley, among them. The Authors Club in the late 1930s was the domain of Rupert Hughes. What a storyteller he was — quite risqué, but funny. He was always followed with a good anecdote by Irwin S. Cobb, also usually rather off-color. As I remember it, Beaman at those meetings was continually table-hopping — greeting, chatting, and seldom eating. He brought Somerset Maugham to one luncheon in 1941, and, as was customary, Maugham was asked to say a few words.

He told of an interesting experience he had had recently. Cuba, it seems, hired an advertising agency to promote the sale of Havana cigars. It proposed a campaign based upon a series of short, short stories in which both a beautiful girl and a windfall of money came as a direct result of smoking a cigar. The agency wrote Maugham inquiring if he'd be willing to write five such sketches for them. He replied that since he wrote to make a living, he was not averse to the proposition and would be willing to write the five stories for $25,000.

This extravagant request, for those days, rather shook the agency, and it wrote back to inquire if the sum suggested might not be a little too high. Maugham replied that since this was to be his first experience in writing commercial advertisements, it might be considered that he was selling his virginity, and he had been told by women of the profession that this was a priceless commodity and worth much more than the usual payment. He hardly expected a reply and never received one.

Miles Standish Slocum, whom we called Ted, probably bought and resold more books than any man who haunted the area of the bookstores. My first recollection of him was when I was working at Vroman's in Pasadena just after college. He was a man who inherited wealth and was just beginning to get interested in collecting. Vroman's was basically a new bookstore, but in those days, in the late 1920s, Herbert Squire and Leslie Hood, who were my bosses, had a few shelves of collector's books — first editions and private presses. Ted Slocum lived in San Marino and naturally first book-hunted at Vroman's. As I remember it, he initially bought a signed limited edition of a set of Rudyard Kipling. It was a hot item at that time, oversubscribed before publication. There were also other popular authors, such as Galsworthy and A.A. Milne, and within a few weeks Ted, in indecision, returned his Kipling for some Galsworthy first editions.

Vroman's limited stock soon lost Slocum to Sixth Street and Dawson's. He kept those stores busy, buying and returning. I best remember when he had almost completed a collection of Ashendene Press books, he tired of them and returned them to Dawson's for credit on future purchases. His interest in particular books was ever-changing, but his devotion was constant. He was one of the first to stimulate book collecting among college students, and since the 1940s, the Slocum Award at Scripps College has been given annually to the senior student who had collected the most outstanding library during her undergraduate years. One of my first books was a commission from him. His nephew, John J. Slocum, had won a literary award at Thatcher School for his poem *The Youth of Hamlet,* and I hand set it and printed twenty-five copies on my Washington handpress, bound it in boards. Its cost could hardly have long curtailed Ted

Slocum's acquisition of books. My charge in 1932 was $134, and my great worry then was that it might be considered excessive.

Just as Ted Slocum had stimulated book collecting at Scripps College through his generous prize, a professor of English literature at Occidental College had managed to do the same many years earlier through sheer enthusiasm. This man, Carlyle F. MacIntyre, introduced me to the bookstores of Sixth Street, as he did my freshman associate, Lawrence Clark Powell. We had a class in English with this man. There were no lazy readers in his class, for he was a tough teacher and force-fed us literature. He loved books and bought them in quantities, haggling and bargaining for every one of them. He'd charge into a Sixth Street bookstore and accumulate a staggering stack. Then he would begin by offering a ridiculous sum for them. The bookseller would inevitably get out a pencil and a sheet of paper and begin to add up the prices he'd put on these books. This meant nothing to MacIntyre, who had studied for his doctor's degree in Europe and was accustomed to bargaining for his purchases. He accumulated books by the shelf. They were not exactly collector's items, they were scholar's books. He'd take them home to read and annotate and then either give or sell them to the Occidental College Library. As he read, he always underlined and wrote marginal comments. Scattered through the Occidental Library is a lot of MacIntyre.

He was a wild, rakish fellow — a poet in the tradition of Byron or Dylan Thomas, loving and drinking through life. He drove a racy Pierce Arrow roadster with the top down — always speeding. Several of us formed a lifelong friendship with him. After stimulating our minds in class, he would grab us off the campus on an afternoon and recklessly race us into town for one of his book-buying sprees. It was this man who introduced me to the buying of books. When I'd accompany him, he'd spot a book at Dawson's or Roger's or one of the other shops and force me to buy it because he thought I should read it.

MacIntyre was both a lyric poet and a playboy. He loved women, and he wrote a continuous diary in verse of his love life. It grew to many volumes. When I was beginning to print, I was also quite enthusiastic about MacIntyre's poetry, and one of my first productions was a small book of his, *The Brimming Cup and Potsherds.* From perhaps a thousand verses he'd written and preserved in a half-dozen thick portfolios, he let me choose a couple of dozen to print. I'm not certain that my choice was the best, but it at least preserved a few of MacIntyre's early lyrics. On New Year's day in 1934, his house and his possessions, including his manuscripts of poems, were swept away in the Montrose flood.

This seemed to have curtailed the creative romantic period of his writing. He continued, partly with a Guggenheim Fellowship, to translate the French and German poets — Goethe, Rilke, Baudelaire, Verlaine, and others — in works that were published as scholarly editions during the remainder of his life.

For a man whose vocabulary, and use of it, was unusually pungent and confounding, his poems had simplicity and a quiet lyric quality. There was a delicacy in them that hardly seemed to fit his boisterous personality. He spent his last decade in Paris, a picturesque Bohemian figure, dominating the conversation at his favorite hangouts, Le Café des Deux Magots and La Flore. Several years ago, in reading an article in *Time* magazine about Paris life, I was surprised to find a couple of paragraphs devoted to the wild American professor from the Left Bank who would race his red roadster through the streets as if he were at Le Mans and could drink all day at his favorite café, talking to a devoted coterie as interestingly about Plato and Socrates as about Sartre and Ginsberg — modern writers whom he detested and about whose talents and antecedents he could be quite caustic. The delicate touch he had in his early lyrics is recalled in this one called "Siesta."

> Brother Junipero,
> His gown girt high,
> Paddled his tired feet
> In a dying creek,
> Ate of dried figs, black olives,
> Spat the seeds
> In a soft cup of earth,
> And buried them.
> Noon fired the trail;
> He lingered on
> And read of Sharon from his book.
> Then with closed eyes
> Dreamed roses,
> Silvery olive trees,
> Fig leaves,
> To the detriment
> Of all the minor prophets.

More typical of the thousand poems that were lost in the flood that destroyed his home was this one:

> When I'm clapped from the sunlight,
> Into dirt
> And no more tilt my bottle
> To your lips,
> While you sit at my feet
> To patch my shirt,
> Singing old ballads,
> Sweet as honey drips;

No one save you
Will mind how we kept house,
Tumbling
Often drunken
Into bed!
You will be quiet
As a padding mouse
And fetch some husband
A shy maidenhead.

The Zamorano Club in its first years had its clubrooms in the once-fashionable Alexandria Hotel at Fifth and Spring streets. When I was a boy this was considered the elite hotel of Los Angeles. When Hollywood became the motion picture capital of the world, the Alexandria also became the headquarters of the men who ran the motion picture business, and most deals were arranged in its bar at the cocktail hour. By the 1930s, the Alexandria had been bypassed. There were newer and bigger hotels in Los Angeles, and Hollywood producers had found more glamorous spots in which to congregate. However, the Zamorano Club found it to be a pleasant central location, and since it was reasonably priced, members leased two rooms on the fourth floor, numbers 484 and 485. They tore out the partitions and panelled the rooms attractively in wood, anticipating a long and pleasant occupancy. With the Alexandria kitchen service available, the Zamoranans felt snug and comfortable. However, they failed to take into consideration the economic trend that had developed since that day in 1929 when the stock market ran into trouble.

C.C. Chapman had bought the hotel in 1930, one of the few bad investments he ever made. He clung to it until 1933 when the earthquake that almost destroyed Long Beach cracked so much of the Alexandria that it became economically expedient to close it. The Zamorano Club found itself locked out and deprived of its handsome rooms.

The club had little trouble in relocating. In those days any hotel would welcome a regularly paying tenant. The University Club offered them delightful rooms on the fourth floor looking out onto Hope Street between Sixth and Wilshire.

This required move turned out to be most fortunate, since it dropped some fifty members of the book-loving Zamorano Club into the vortex of the booksellers area. Each Wednesday noon after their luncheon, during which they had whetted one another's appetite for acquisitions, they would rush out, with gentlemanly reticence, of course, to scavenge Sixth Street and Dawson's and to gloat if they managed to find an undiscovered sleeper.

The first president and the man most responsible for the Zamorano Club was Arthur M. Ellis. He was a catalyst of book clubs and a stimulant to printers and collectors of California material. In 1927 W. Irving Way was peddling books in Los Angeles, selling many of the treasures he had acquired during the years in Chicago when he was a prime publisher with the firm of Way and Williams. He had great acumen and taste. In 1895 he was one of the first intuitive publishers to recognize the talents of the young Bruce Rogers, and he entrusted Rogers to design a book, *The Banquet of Plato,* translated by Percy Bysshe Shelley. He also recognized the great contribution that William Morris and his Kelmscott Press had made to the art of printing in acknowledging and reviving the quality of the books of earlier centuries.

Way, with a bit of American soft sell, induced Morris to print for him an edition of Rossetti's *Hand and Soul.* It was a remarkable accomplishment for several reasons. Morris's Kelmscott

Press books were about the most sought after collector's items in England at the time, with every book oversubscribed upon being announced. Also, while Rossetti and Morris had been the closest of friends during the Pre-Raphaelite period, it is now quite generally known that Morris realized that Rossetti and Jane Morris, his wife, had had an affair of long duration. Morris was either forgiving or indifferent since he agreed to print Rossetti's book for Irving Way, the only one of his books done for an American publisher.

In 1927 Way was in Los Angeles, impoverished and living on the residue of the books he had accumulated and saved. I remember one particular book he sold to Jake Zeitlin, *That Endeth Never* by Hildegarde Flanner. It was one of the most handsomely printed books I have ever seen. I hesitated in buying it, for two good reasons. At the time I couldn't afford it and also I was superstitious enough to give credence to Porter Garnett's malediction in his explicit and lengthy colophon:

"Because this story, in manuscript form, was a *gift;* because the printed copies are also to be gifts; because this book, done in the fifty-fifth year of my life, is the first to be composed in type entirely by my own hands; and because the making of it has been a labor of love, it is my wish that NO COPY OF THIS BOOK SHALL EVER BE BOUGHT, SOLD, OR BARTERED either separately or a part of a collection or library.

"Whosoever — impelled by that most contemptible of human passions, the desire of gain — shall, *at any time,* purchase, sell, or exchange a copy of this book, will brand himself forthwith as *without conscience or honour,* and upon him, upon his children and his children's children shall rest, for ever and ever, my *malediction.* O good and beautiful Proserpina, or Salvia, shouldst thou prefer, mayest thou wrest away from the mercenary wretch who buys or sells or barters this book his health, body, complexion, strength, and faculties, and consign him to thy husband, Pluto, that, in the Land of the Departed, he may suffer the combined agonies of Ixion, Sisyphus, Tantalus, and the other departed shades. Suffer him to collect, at great cost, the worthless 'firsts' of ephemeral Nobodies. Mayest thou consign him to the quartian, tertian, and daily fevers, to war and wrestle with till they snatch away his very soul. Suffer that all his 'a.l.s's' and inscriptions shall be forgeries. Mayest thou, Proserpina, or Acherusia, shouldst thou prefer, summon for me the three-headed dog, Cerberus, to tear out the heart of him, and mayest thou pledge thyself to give to thy faithful hound three offerings — dates, figs, and a black swine — when he shall have performed his task. Suffer his 'rare items' to become drugs on the market. To thee, Proserpina, Acherusia, I give his head, his brow and eyebrows, eyelids and pupils; I give thee his ears, nose, nostrils, tongue, lips, and teeth, so he may not speak his pain; his neck, shoulders, arms and fingers, so he may not aid himself; his breast, liver, heart, and lungs, so he may not locate his pain; his bowels, belly, navel, and flanks, so he may not sleep the sleep of health; his thighs, legs, knees, shanks, feet, ankles, toes, and toenails, so he may not stand of his own strength. Suffer his 'unique copies' to be stolen, his private press books, his 'limited editions' (ridiculous though such things be), and books, with highfaluting colophons and 'printer's notes' (such as this), to be destroyed by fire. And, O proud and lovely Proserpina, Salvia, Acherusia, may he be condemned, during the whole of his miserable life, while awaiting thy dark and dire ministrations, to consort only with people who are — dull." Most printers don't so restrict prospective purchasers of their books.

Irving Way was quite destitute when Will Clary, Gay Beaman, and Arthur Ellis gathered with him at a luncheon and conceived the idea of a club for bibliophiles. Way was to be the librarian and was to receive some compensation. His portrait was painted and hung in the club room. Unfortunately he lived but a short time after the beginning of the Zamorano Club that was to help sustain him.

After Arthur Ellis had initiated the Zamorano Club, I understand that he suggested to several San Franciscans the formation of a similar organization, and the Roxburghe Club was formed in that city in 1928. He spoke at their meeting on October 8 of that year. He also prompted the creation of the Rounce and Coffin Club, which was conceived and born in 1931. He wanted everyone he knew to be involved with books and the love of them.

His primary interest was Californiana, but his secondary, and eventually most important one was printing. In back of his house were two little buildings, one of which contained a Colt's Armory press on which he printed a few books by himself. He also cast type by hand and attempted to make paper. His interest in printing induced him to order an Albion handpress from the Caslon Company in England. Oddly enough, in 1929, a new handpress was still available from this venerable English firm. Introducing it into the United States created a problem which Arthur Ellis had not anticipated. He was an eminent lawyer, a conservative citizen, a longtime resident of Los Angeles, but this strange importation made him quite suspect. The United States Treasury Department assigned a man to check if this could be the nucleus of a new counterfeit ring. Ellis was able to convince him that he was only an ambitious amateur printer, and when he was unable to untangle and describe the various segments of this so-called Albion handpress, they became convinced that he would not be a man capable of duplicating the currency of the United States.

Ellis was confounded by this arrangement of contorted iron

that he had bought, and he called upon Jake Zeitlin to help him out of his dilemma. Jake took one look at it and decided that an admission of ignorance was his best answer. He in turn called upon Grant Dahlstrom for help, and Grant, with knowledge acquired at the Carnegie Institute of Technology, agreed to help erect the press. When he and Jake arrived at the Ellis home the next Sunday morning, they were amazed to find the erection substantially completed. Ellis, always impatient, hadn't been able to wait and, with a block and tackle he'd attached to a ceiling beam, had managed to maneuver the heavy pieces into place. Many of the early keepsakes of the Zamorano Club were printed on this press. Jake Zeitlin, or it may have been Dahlstrom, suggested it be called the Ampersand Press — a most appropriate name.

The Wednesday noon exodus of Zamorano Club members from their new quarters at the University Club was usually led by rotund Henry Wagner, who waddled down Flower to Sixth Street to pay some attention to the booksellers located there and then turned the corner to visit Dawson's. This was a ritual. Following would be Hodge, Cowan, J. Gregg Layne, Carl Wheat, Don Hill, Will Robinson, Will Clary, and Homer Crotty. In later years there was an increasing cavalcade, including Robert Woods, Ed Ainsworth, Ben Kirby, George Fullerton, Lawrence Powell, John Goodman, and almost every member of the club who didn't have to rush back to an office to make a living.

The enthusiasm of these men for books, and the opportunity to talk about books led them to gather on many other occasions and places which I am happy to remember.

Carl I. Wheat, who worked his way through Pomona College and on to San Francisco, returned to Los Angeles in 1934. Previously he had been Master of the Press of the Roxburghe Club for the first five years after its founding. In Los Angeles he quickly became involved. The Historical Society of Southern California had published an *Annual* since its founding in the 1880s. He became its editor and convinced the editorial board, which consisted of Frederick Webb Hodge, J. Gregg Layne, and Henry R. Wagner, that henceforth the publication should be a quarterly, which it has been since. The first issue should be a treasured one for those who have a copy. Paul Landacre, one of the most talented of American wood engravers, made three woodcuts for this edition.

Carl Wheat brought great stuff into the *Quarterly*, editorially and pictorially, including a reproduction of the Ord survey map of Los Angeles of 1849 and the drawing by H.M.T. Powell of Los Angeles in March 1850, neither of which showed a trace of smog.

He also introduced the order of E Clampus Vitus into southern California, which he liked to call the "cow counties." He had found in his studies of early California newspapers, references to a fun-loving group of miners using this preposterous sobriquet. He revived the order in San Francisco, and when he moved to Los Angeles he installed the Platrix chapter, which has survived in a lusty fashion to this day.

Along with Carl Wheat, the Californiana buffs — Gregg Layne, Pink Bynum, Bob Woods, Rowe Sandersen, and Will Robinson — met quite regularly at La Golondrina on Olvera Street for margaritas and lunch. I went to these gatherings often enough to know that while the conversation might seem light and frivolous, there was always an exchange of information. Between these men was represented an encyclopedia of local and western history, which when combined with the knowledge of Cowan, Wagner, Hanna, and Hodge, concentrated an incredible amount of information about this area, which was dispensed with generous and pleasant abandon.

Bynum had been the field representative of the Huntington Library for many years before becoming assistant to Robert Gordon Sproul, president of the University of California. He combed the state, uncovering historical material in attics and trunks, inducing sweet old ladies to give their treasures to the university for their preservation. It was a pleasant way of life, this historical sleuthing. But while on the road, he also became interested in the food of the land. He sniffed out agreeable places in which to dine — Basque, Mexican, Armenian, Chinese. He came to know the select spots up and down the state. And while involved in this engrossing hobby, he also became interested in the wines of California, especially those of the Napa and Sonoma Valleys, where he would sneak whenever he could find the excuse of an historical lead.

He was endowed with a mellow, twinkling charm that endeared him to most of the people with whom he was negotiating for their family letters, diaries, and pictures. He was a superb storyteller and limericist — I've heard him go on for an hour without repeating himself. But his greatest asset was his nose. He could sniff the bouquet of a wine and identify the grape — a pinot noir, a cabernet sauvignon, a zinfandel. He could often identify the winery from which it came — Louis Martini, Inglenook, Buena Vista. In his later years he seldom drank hard liquor, preferring to sniff, sip, and build his memory of wine's subtle variations.

While he preferred the greater wines of the northern regions, he enjoyed all California wines — and especially the game of identifying and classifying them. Occasionally he'd arrange for a luncheon and a special tasting, which would bring out bottles and barrels a winery didn't ordinarily dispense. He was a careful man, and to preclude any trouble he'd include Sheriff Gene Biscailuz and Dr. Marcus Crahan for protection, both physical and medical. One of these occasions happened at the San Gabriel Winery, whose vineyards and buildings are now buried in memory and urban development. We tasted a variety of sherries, had lunch with wines, and then indulged ourselves in a long-hoarded brandy. They only had a few bottles left but we drained them. I managed to get home with only a bent fender, and there were other casualties.

Bob Woods, however, woke up the next morning with a strange gadget. He had admired it hanging on the wall of the winery and somehow acquired it, together with the following explanation of its purpose and use:

"Should you not be familiar with the identity of the enclosed device, it is known as a BULL SNUBBER. The specimen, from which this copy was made was discovered after considerable travel and research in the cow country. In the days when open range was the rule, the tough old range bulls had plenty of room to roam and gave the cow hands less trouble. After the cattle men started fencing it off in lots of, say, 100,000 acres, the bulls began to show touches of claustrophobia and became more ornery. It was then that the BULL SNUBBER grew popular and often was carried on the belt by the cow pokes. Encountering a difficult critter, the cow boy would herd him over toward the barbed wire fence and maneuver him into position close to the wire. Seated on his pony, facing the bull, the cow hand would slip from the saddle on the off side while the bull was watching the pony. Drawing the BULL SNUBBER from his belt he ran quickly to the rear of the bull. Speed, dexterity and fine co-ordination were required now. A quick forward thrust of the SNUBBER impaled the bull effectively. Holding the loop and pin in one hand, before the critter could recover from his surprise, the cow poke seized the top wire of the fence with the other hand and snapped the pin around it. He could then advance to the front end of the bull with perfect equanimity and even pat the animal's nose on the way by. The bull might talk back some but he paid no attention and was now free to mount his pony and proceed with the business of the day . . . After a proper cooling off period the cow hand might return and release the bull with an extractor . . . usually from the other side of the fence . . . on account of possible difference of opinion."

Woods always planned, because of the evident usefulness of the device, to have copies made as a keepsake for a Zamorano-Roxburghe gathering, but time crept too fast for him.

Not all collectors read their books. Robert Woods not only collected avidly, but read thoroughly and remembered. His collection is now at the University of Alberta, but once it served us well. For years Will Robinson, Bob, and I gathered for lunch on Tuesdays. We'd start with a couple of Manhattans (Bob would have four) and we'd fall into a lively discussion of books and sex. We wandered through the restaurants of Los Angeles and at every one of them, Bob, with a twinkle in his eye and a sprightly touch of suggestiveness in his greeting, captivated every waitress we ever had. They'd hover around, give him a pat and sometimes a kiss. Bob enjoyed himself. When the discussion turned to books he was all information, and if it was of a particular subject or person, he'd arrive next week with a bundle of books from his seemingly limitless library to more completely illustrate or prove a point. Some of the best parties I remember were given in the patio of his hillside house on Briarcliffe Road. He'd gather all of the Californiana crowd. Wagner and Hodge would relax and expound. J. Frank Dobie came from Texas a couple of times, saying they were the best parties he'd attended east or west. I can well understand his appreciation, with a dozen or two of our local collectors and historians on hand with whom to talk. He'd never been surrounded by such wealth anywhere. And then, of course, Woods had caches here and there of old rum, tequila, bourbon, and Scotch to accelerate the conversation.

It must appear from my remarks that the book collectors of Los Angeles were avid for food and drink. While not universally true, there seems to have been such a tendency, though it may possibly reflect the recollections most indelible in my own memories.

After Carl Wheat left Los Angeles for Washington, D.C., the luncheons at La Golondrina dwindled to Bynum, Woods, Robinson, and Layne. The spot began to lose its appeal, and Woods discovered El Cholo, a Mexican restaurant on Western Avenue near Olympic. The Thursday luncheons were transferred, and for perhaps fifteen years until his death, Woods presided at a table there, kidded the waitresses, and enjoyed tortillas, enchiladas, and frijoles refritos. For a few years Bynum, Woods, Robinson, Layne, and I were the nucleus. After Layne's death and Bynum's retirement to his favored Napa Valley, Bob Woods lured a new group of collectors to these luncheons; a group that adopted the name of The Wine, Food, and Wench Society. John Goodman, George Fullerton, Webster Jones, Will Robinson, John Urabec, Gordon Holmquist, Frank Dolley, and Andrew Horn were the most frequent visitors. Woods was the constant one, arriving punctually each Thursday noon to await the next arrival. There was much interplay of conversation with the attractive waitresses, and food and talk. He always regretted breakup time. In the days when he was still managing his apartment house, he'd sometimes lure a few of us back to taste a special wine he had. He was constantly picking up good wines at Balzer's or Converse's and at one time put down a very creditable cellar of some of the outstanding Burgundies and Bourdeaux. He had some great 1929s, such as Romanée Conti and Chateau Lafite Rothschild, which he let age in his cellar and joyously often indulged friends with a tasting.

For a special occasion he brought out a few bottles of these greatest of French wines. They seemed to lack most of the qualities we usually attribute to a good, if not great, wine. A few days later I was given a half dozen bottles of these fantastic vintages, which I savored and treasured until I served them. Bob's wine cellar was next to his furnace, and over the years the wines had become thoroughly cooked.

Gregg Layne, along with Will Robinson, had the most intimate and detailed knowledge of anyone of Los Angeles history. It seems a pity that a whole lifetime's accumulation of information such as his should be lost with him. As far as I know he left no notes or jottings and very few written articles. Will Robinson has mentioned to me that one of his great regrets is not having made notes of the conversations he had with Gregg about local history. His knowledge was incredible. I remember a Zamorano meeting at which he talked about the streets of early Los Angeles, and pausing for every street number, he recalled that building's history, its inhabitants, and an interesting anecdote of early happenings there.

Layne's knowledge of Californiana gave him an advantage over most of the local booksellers. He accumulated one outstanding library that he sold to Mrs. Edward L. Doheny, who in turn gave it to the University of Southern California. With nary a moment's hesitation he began another, which eventually was purchased by UCLA. For most of his life he sold draftsmen's materials, but upon retiring he was retained by the Los Angeles Department of Water and Power to write a history of the development of water in the Los Angeles area. He worked five years on it and, later, often remarked that it was the best unpublished $30,000 history ever locally written. The reluctance of the department to publish it is beclouded in politics and finances.

Larry Powell grabbed him for the UCLA Library when he left city employment, and the final year of his life was most enjoyably spent ferreting out the invaluable books of the Robert Cowan Library. UCLA had bought Cowan's collection of Californiana and, following the then usual procedure, had not kept them intact and segregated within their Californiana or Special Collections. They had been distributed into the general collection of a million books. Gregg's last days were happy ones, ferreting out these treasures and reassembling a rare library.

Zeitlin's Bookstore was the first to abandon the area of Sixth Street, moving in the 1930s to the old carriage house of the Earl house on Wilshire Boulevard, an extension of the Otis Art Institute. Others left as their ramshackle quarters were demolished and banks and high-rise buildings took over. Dawson was ousted from his corner at Wilshire and Grand, but he hung to the area on Figueroa near Sixth for several years when this building, too, surrendered to progress. Now there is not a remnant, not a trace left in the area of those bookstores which so well served the book collectors of Los Angeles during the 1930s and 1940s.

Few from those days have survived. Others have come but are scattered like leaves in a wind about a city that has lost its central core.

# 2

## JAKE ZEITLIN
### WHEN HE WAS JOYOUS YOUNG

---

*The late Jake Zeitlin was the dean of booksellers in Los Angeles, where he kept a lively shop for sixty years. He was the catalyst responsible for much of the artistic and literary resurgence during the 1930s. His bookstore was the favored hangout for artists, authors, and printers, who were always encouraged by Jake's enthusiasm and advice.*

---

HERE I AM REMEMBERING DAYS sixty years past. I was in college then, and although Jake Zeitlin was only three years older than I, I looked upon him with veneration as one of the older generation. He was a published poet and an established businessman operating his own bookshop.

It was not sumptuous; it was probably the smallest bookshop in existence. Established in the back stairway of a derelict building that may once have been a brothel, it was located (optimistically) on Hope Street across from the Bible Institute, sandwiched between the public library and Sixth Street, then the "bookseller's row" of Los Angeles. The stairs had been boarded up, leaving the door and about ten feet of entrance lined with shelves to carry a meager assortment of books. A paunchy customer could never have been accommodated.

It wasn't long before he outgrew these cramped quarters and moved around the corner to slightly larger quarters at 705$^{1}/_{2}$

44

West Sixth Street along with dozens of other antiquarian dealers — or, as we termed them in those days, secondhand booksellers — who lined the street in rickety buildings.

Larry Powell — before he became Lawrence Clark Powell — and I would often ditch classes at Occidental College to spend an afternoon sifting through books along the street, always ending up at Jake's shop. There were always a half dozen writers and artists there, attracted by Jake's magnetism.

Here we met an array of creative men, many of whom became lifelong friends — authors Louis Adamic, Merle Armitage, Paul Jordan-Smith, Carey McWilliams, Phil Townsend Hanna, and W. W. Robinson; artists Paul Landacre, Fletcher Martin, and Edward Weston; and the young printers, Grant Dahlstrom and Saul Marks. Several of these, along with Jake, decided to pool their talents and publish a monthly magazine called *Opinion* wherein they could freely express their opinions without editorial interference. It lasted for a year.

Of course, we occasionally bought a book from Jake, although we spent most of our time browsing through the press books in such vogue with collectors during the 1920s. Jake was interested in fine printing and usually had a gathering of books printed by the Grabhorns and Bruce Rogers, along with English imports from the Nonesuch and Golden Cockerel presses. These books appealed to me.

Jake grew up in Fort Worth, Texas, where his family had a vinegar factory. Jake was precocious. Besides working in the vinegar factory, he wrote poetry, winning a statewide prize, and reviewed books and entertainments for the local newspaper.

This aroused some interest in books for Jake, but it was the inexplicable arrival of Ben Abramson and another antiquarian bookseller from Chicago who took temporary jobs in the vinegar factory that lured Jake into his lifetime profession. The two booksellers talked about nothing except rare books all day long, and Jake eagerly listened.

After they left Jake slung his guitar over his shoulder and with a suitcase heavy with books started to hitchhike to California, bound for a new career away from the vinegar factory. He arrived penniless, dusty, and hungry.

As I recall his telling me, he first got a job washing dishes in a cafeteria in order to eat. Next he found temporary employment shoveling fertilizer in the Doheny garden. Years later, in different circumstances, he was to sell to the Countess Estelle Doheny some of the priceless books and manuscripts recently auctioned by Christie's at fantastic prices.

As soon as he could manage it, Jake got a job in the book department of Bullock's Department Store. Here he accumulated some selling experience and the wherewithal to commence on his own. He began with only his old suitcase filled with books lent to him by Dawson and other sympathetic dealers, and he peddled them at the motion picture studios and wherever he could find a potential collector.

When Ernest Maggs visited Los Angeles in the late 1920s with a trunkful of treasures, he was so impressed with the young and congenial Jake that he left his unsold books with him to sell as he could, on commission. This was Jake's actual initiation into the rare book business.

While he was still living in Fort Worth, Jake had interviewed Carl Sandburg and had later helped him arrange some poetry readings. Sandburg liked the young man and later wrote a nice foreword for Jake's first book of poems, *For Whispers and Chants*, beautifully printed by the Grabhorn Press of San Francisco.

They continued to correspond, and on the day I rushed to tell Jake that I had enrolled in trade school to learn how to become a printer, he had received a letter from Sandburg enclosing a new poem of his entitled "Soo Line Sonata." Jake suggested that I might like to print it. I jubilantly took it and stumbled through my first frustrating experience in printing as I pieced together the letters and words of the poem.

After I had struggled through setting the six pages of text, I decided it needed decoration and proceeded with a heavy hand. Then I proudly took my "masterpiece" to show Jake. He went into mild shock, blinking his eyes in disbelief, and suggested that we forget the project. Also he'd had a subsequent note from Sandburg telling him that he didn't want the poem published and that he'd send him another, "M'Liss & Louie," which I printed a few months later after I'd had a bit more experience.

Sorrowfully, I took the proofs of "Soo Line Sonata" home with me to ponder Jake's disapproval. I began to understand, and the next day I removed all the excessive decoration and reproofed the pages unadorned. I had had my first lesson in typographic taste. I showed Jake the new setup and was pleased that he liked it. Although he couldn't publish it, he suggested that I print five copies for the record.

I continued to print some small booklets of poems by other of my favorite poets, Robinson Jeffers, Archibald MacLeish, and Louise Bogan, before I decided that I'd go to Paris in hope of working with the artist/printer François-Louis Schmied. To help me out, Jake authorized me to buy books for him at my discretion, for which he'd pay me a small commission.

I now often wonder how I had the youthful brashness to travel overseas unannounced and expect to get a job with one of the world's greatest printers, but I did. After a year I got a cable from Jake offering me a job in his shop for $100 a month. It was too good an offer to refuse, and I returned to California in the fall of 1931, at the peak of the Depression, to work for Jake.

I lasted just about two months before Jake decided I'd make a better printer than a bookseller, and so, early in 1932 The Ward Ritchie Press came into existence in a barn behind my family home in South Pasadena with a bare minimum of equipment, a Washington handpress and three or four cases of type.

One happy event during my short tenure in Jake's shop was the formation of the Rounce and Coffin Club, which for the past fifty years has sponsored the annual Western Books Show. The Zamorano Club had been formed by a group of older bibliophiles in 1928, three years earlier. We "youngsters" felt left out, so one October evening while loitering around the bookshop, Jake and I, along with Gregg Anderson and Grant Dahlstrom, decided to form our own club. We gathered a friendly group and had many boisterous meetings until we all grew older and became more sedate in the manner of the older Zamorano Club.

Jake had been dabbling in publishing under the imprint of the Primavera Press. Once I had some printing equipment, he commissioned me to print some of his books. They were mostly vanity books. Jake yearned to establish a more legitimate publishing house and asked me and Phil Townsend Hanna, the editor of *Westways* magazine, to join him.

Jake became the major partner in charge of sales and promotion, Hanna acted as editor, and I handled production. Later on we added Carey McWilliams as our attorney, Lawrence Clark Powell as shipping clerk, and Cornelis Groenewegen as accountant. Despite the Depression, the Primavera Press managed to last until 1936, publishing many worthy titles.

Its demise was probably best for all of us. We could once again devote all of our energies to our own businesses. Also, there was another positive factor. Next door to Jake's third shop, which had been handsomely designed for him by Lloyd Wright, the son of Frank Lloyd Wright, there was a small bar. A generous martini was served there at the Depression-time price of 15 cents. We always preceded our monthly strategy meetings with a visit to this convenient establishment. Phil Hanna had an amazing capacity for martinis, and their flow never seemed to cease. Our health revived somewhat after the demise of the Press.

Jake had five different shops during his long career as a Los Angeles bookseller. The first three were in the vicinity of "bookseller's row" in downtown Los Angeles, then a rather seedy area of reasonable rents, now the high-rise district of high rents that have driven the booksellers to the outskirts. In the 1930s there was a constant flow of browsers wandering among the dozen or more shops on the street. It was friendly and clublike, almost small-townish in the certainty of finding many friendly faces during a visit.

Jake's good friend Louis Samuel was not so fortunate. His Penguin Bookshop was some distance out on Wilshire Boulevard. The arrival of a browser in his shop was an occasion of importance, and Louis would hover with anticipation when one would arrive.

On one quiet day a lone man appeared, and Louis flooded him with books to peruse. When he showed him a copy of the Lakeside Press edition of *Moby Dick* illustrated by Rockwell Kent, the stranger casually remarked, "You like my book?" Samuel was ecstatic at having Rockwell Kent in his grasp and immediately asked him if he might be free for a little gathering that evening. Kent was, and Louis immediately got on the phone to call Jake and a few others to gather at his home in Eagle Rock to meet Rockwell Kent. Samuel picked up some bottles and drove Kent up to his hideaway. It was a convivial evening. Kent didn't have much to say, but he enjoyed himself.

For some reason Jake became suspicious. He had never met Kent before, but he had corresponded with him and had a show of Kent prints in the small gallery attached to his bookshop. Jake phoned a friend who had known Kent and asked what he looked like. He was told that Kent was medium-tall and almost completely bald. The man at the party was short with a mop of hair. Jake didn't want to spoil the party so he kept quiet. Later Louis asked Jake if he'd mind dropping Kent off at his hotel in Hollywood as it was more or less on Jake's way home. Jake agreed, and while in the car Jake accused the man of being an imposter. The only answer was, "What impertinence," and the trip continued in total silence.

It turned out this man had been a groom on Kent's estate at Ausable Falls, New York, and thus knew enough about Kent and his work to impersonate him. The imposter's real name was Mike Gergeson. Before working for Kent he had knocked around Greenwich Village in New York, affably crashing parties under the guise of being Prince Michael Romanoff.

After the exposure of his Kent subterfuge, he reassumed his Prince Michael Romanoff pose and was embraced by the Hollywood elite, resulting in the financing of his Romanoff's restaurant in Beverly Hills, which became the most exclusive place to eat and to be seen in southern California. He and Jake eventually became quite good friends, and Jake was impressed by his intellectual curiosity and the books Mike bought from him.

Not too long after this bizarre affair, I read that the real Rockwell Kent was planning a lecture tour that would bring him West. He had belonged to the same college fraternity as Larry Powell and I, and we cautiously wrote him and asked if he'd consider giving the annual Phi Gamma Delta lecture at Occidental College. He agreed.

Jake, Larry, and I attended his lecture and afterward drove him up to my print shop studio for a dinner of spaghetti and quantities of red wine. He regaled us with tales of his undergraduate pranks and his adventures in Alaska and Newfoundland, among others. The wine had made us friends, and Jake suggested that the Primavera Press would like to print Larry's recently completed thesis on Robinson Jeffers if Rockwell would illustrate it. Kent took another long swig of wine and agreed.

I made some hurried sketches of what we'd need, including pictorial initials for each chapter opening. Of course Kent wanted to know what the letters would be. Fearful that if I delayed he might change his mind, I wrote down a dozen or so random letters that popped into my mind. Kent stuffed my notes in his pockets, and, surprisingly enough, in a couple of weeks a package of drawings arrived from him. Powell considerately rewrote all of the opening paragraphs of the chapters in his book to accommodate my haphazard choices of initial letters.

And then one day, not long after, a practical schoolteacher from Kansas walked into Jake's shop looking for a summer job. Jake had hardly taken one glance at her before he told me that this was the girl he was going to marry.

The next evening Jake and I went to a bibulous dinner of the Wine and Food Society immaculately dressed in formal tuxedos. Afterward Jake decided he wanted to see this girl he'd decided to marry. She had left her address with him when applying for the job. We eventually found the place, a two-story apartment building with a vacant lot on the side. The hour was quite late, and the entrance door was firmly locked, possibly to protect the virtue of the working girls living there from prowling lotharios the likes of us.

Jake was not to be daunted. We retreated to the vacant lot to gather a supply of pebbles and began methodically to pepper each window on the side of the building while loudly shouting, "Josephine, Josephine." Somehow we aroused some wrath among the occupants, without getting a response from our

Josephine. We retreated ingloriously when we heard police sirens, fearing that our enthusiastic efforts to find Josephine might have resulted in an alert to the authorities.

Josephine showed up at Jake's bookshop the next day, wondering what all of the commotion had been at her apartment house the previous evening.

And so Jake married her, depriving a small school in Kansas of its talented teacher. That young girl, Josephine Ver Brugge, a stalwart Dutch girl, settled Jake down and converted the playboy of the book world into the honored and mature merchant bookman we now remember with such admiration and affection.

# 3

## PAUL LANDACRE
### ARTIST AND WOOD ENGRAVER

*From the year of 1932 when the Ward Ritchie Press was established with the printing of Jeffers' essay, "First Book," done for* The Colophon *with a Landacre engraving, this artist has been responsible for illustrating over a dozen of Ritchie's books. This partially tells of his struggles to perfection.*

HERE IS THE STORY of Paul Landacre, born in Columbus, Ohio, on July 9, 1893. His story is one of triumph and heartbreak. A handsome boy and athletically inclined, he was captain of his high school track team and the premier miler in Ohio, easily winning the state meet. As an athlete of great promise, he was wooed by many colleges, but decided to attend his hometown Ohio State University, from which his father had graduated. As a freshman in 1914 and 1915, he continued to run and win. Then he was struck with an infection which baffled the doctors and left him crippled for life and understandably depressed. He quit school in 1916 to recuperate. As therapy he began to draw, a pursuit for which he had always had a natural talent. He had passed many of his science courses more because of the drawings with which he illustrated his papers than for his comprehension of the subject.

He made the move from Ohio to San Diego, California,

hoping to make a living as a commercial artist. Being a stubborn perfectionist and ploddingly slow, he probably was not too successful. But in one of the advertising agencies for which he did an occasional job, he met a copywriter named Margaret McCreery, to whom he was attracted. She was a hearty girl, lovely and sweet-tempered, and Landacre was quite handsome despite his infirmities.

They were soon married, and theirs was a love that lasted in intimate harmony for almost forty years. She devoted her life to him and had such faith in his talents that she insisted that he attend art school and dedicate his time to fine art while she continued working to support him. Gradually he discovered that his talents were best suited to engraving on wood, and as the years passed, he became one of America's finest engravers.

Once Paul was asked what Margaret did. He thought for a moment and answered, "She takes care of the correspondence, answers the telephone, is chancellor of the exchequer, drives me to and from wherever I have to go, helps push the lever of the press when I have to print a large block, delivers prints, checks the manuscript when I am illustrating a book, keeps house, and is an excellent cook. And then she acts as critic and as a balance wheel; she boosts my morale when I am discouraged and calms me if I get too excited over my work at the wrong time. Any art coming out of this studio is a dual production for sure."

She did much more than this. She warmed his frail body at night. She built his confidence. She worked to support him while he was learning the greatness which was to be his. It was as close and beautiful an association as I have known.

A good many years ago I thought I'd write something about the Landacres. I began one night: "Paul and Margaret Landacre live a couple of hills over from Silver Lake, which separates us. Their house, like a redwood dam, lies on a steep slope, backing up a few small areas of flat ground where flowers grow and where they plant the tallest stand of corn in the West. A twisting dirt road encompasses their place on three sides. It is barely wide enough for a car to navigate and presents a serious problem if and when another car should approach. But this happens so seldom that the problem has never become acute. When it rains, friends worry lest the Landacres's house will slide down into the valley below. And when, with the summer, the spring grass has become brown and tangled beneath the oaks and eucalyptus trees, and the lot cleaners began to burn off the hills, they ask if the Landacres could possibly have survived. Only the initiated can ever find their place. It even took the assessor years to find it. They seem not to live where they do, and, according to the map, the streets that should take you to them don't. Even the postman was perplexed and, after years of confusion, had to give them a new street number. Taxi drivers had given up years earlier trying to take people to see them.

"And yet up there the stars are very close; the breezes bring nostalgic music from the trains in the valley down below, and the lights of the city make a varicolored pattern that the Landacres love and you would also love." That was as far as I wrote.

I regret that I didn't continue. Now I have to rely upon my memory of events that go back over sixty years. In 1928 Margaret was working for Jake Zeitlin. Paul, who had become discouraged with commercial art, began, with Margaret's encouragement, to experiment, first with etchings and then with gingerly cut linoleum blocks. He did a self-portrait and a portrait of the then-young Jake Zeitlin, both of which were quite successful, before he began experimenting with engraving on wood. Several years later he wrote of these endeavors, "My study of wood engraving was conducted almost entirely by trial and error, as my only formal art education consisted of some intermittent classes in life drawing. At that time much less wood engraving was being done and there was no one in this vicinity to advise me. It was also difficult to find any books on the subject, which necessitated my digging it out for myself."

He learned remarkably fast and well, though his technique was awkward. I had worked with some professional engravers in Paris and had observed the way they held their tools and the ease with which they could make their cuts. I was astonished to see the laborious technique that Paul had improvised, but it worked for him with results close to perfection.

Zeitlin's little bookshop couldn't have been over 150 square feet, with a shipping area and a small room to one side where Margaret Landacre took care of accounting and correspondence. The shop was crowded with modern press books from Nonesuch, Golden Cockerel, Grabhorn, Bruce Rogers, and other presses that had proliferated in those "Golden Twenties" of printing. These books were illustrated by the likes of Eric Gill, Rockwell Kent, Robert Gibbings, and Valenti Angelo. Zeitlin was a poet at heart, a bookseller by profession, and an art lover. He withheld one wall from his rows of books to display the works of some of the artists he admired. Here he gave Landacre's engravings their first showing. As a young fellow recently out of college, I remember the excitement of buying one of those prints for what was for me the tremendous sum of ten dollars.

That must have been in late 1929 or early 1930. Those early engravings, cut mostly on uniform rectangular blocks with rather coarse strokes, were effective renditions of scenes Landacre had sketched on trips to the desert around Indio, Malibu, and the mountains of Big Sur and Monterey. Most of these early landscape blocks were reproduced in a beautiful book, *California Hills and Other Wood Engravings,* published by Bruce McCallister in 1931. It was printed directly from the original blocks and almost matched the quality of the prints that Landacre pulled himself on his Washington handpress.

This was a beautiful press, much more decorative than most Washington presses. Willard Morgan discovered it in rusty pieces in the mining ghost town of Bodie. By local tradition, which Paul would hardly dispute, it had once been used by Mark Twain, but that is quite apocryphal. Morgan deposited it with Landacre, who lovingly scraped it, painted it, and reassembled it. It was a large press that was difficult for Paul to handle alone, but he would pull mightily from the front while Margaret pushed with all her strength from the back. Together they were able to hand-print editions of fifty or sixty copies from Paul's blocks. It often took them several weeks to complete even a portion of that number. Sometimes the full edition was never completed, as they would print copies only when they had an order. When, on several occasions, Paul was commissioned to do a print in larger quantities, as he was for the members of the Philadelphia Print Club, he'd have Saul Marks, Grant Dahlstrom, or me print the edition.

For ink he used a stiff, heavy-bodied lithographer's woodcut black without dryer. He once wrote, "The non-drying quality is something of a personal preference. It allows the ink to be removed from the block with ease, even after standing on the roller or on the ink slab. This is an advantage while pulling trial proofs or printing a few prints on successive days — obviating the necessity of continually washing up. Moreover, the stiff or heavy-bodied quality is necessary in printing large areas of black in conjunction with fine, delicate lines. The stiffer the ink, the better, though it takes hand rolling and much pressure to use it."

Jake Zeitlin, in addition to his bookselling, decided to expand his publishing activities under the imprint of the Primavera Press and invited several of us to work with him. Jake had arranged for Saul Marks' Plantin Press to print Alexandre Dumas' *A Gil Blas in California*. I was designated to design it, and we induced Landacre to illustrate it with engravings, including a large map of the California gold regions for the frontispiece and the dust jacket. For decoration on the title page, I asked Paul to adapt the printer's mark of Espinosa, a bull and anchor that had been the first printer's mark used on the American continent. I later adopted it for my own pressmark.

After Paul had finished the twenty-two engravings for *Gil Blas*, I persuaded him to cut some ornaments for me to use in a small book of poems I had written and was planning to get out for Christmas. Both books were typographically successful and were selected by the American Institute of Graphic Arts for inclusion in the Fifty Books of the Year 1934. Two other books illustrated by Paul had been included in earlier selections, his own *California Hills* and Edward Doro's *The Boar and Shibboleth*. Paul illustrated about a dozen books for me. I no longer remember our financial arrangements, but I am certain that not much money changed hands. We were then in the midst of the Great Depression, and there wasn't much money around.

At that time I had an old ranch house on the eastern edge of Hollywood where William S. Hart had lived as a foreman when he was working cattle in the hills around what is now known as Silver Lake. Early movie producers, desperately needing a cowboy, had picked him up and made him an early star despite his lack of acting ability. The original Disney Studios were just up the street, and most of the artists lived and loved in the neighborhood. Our house was on a hillside of Griffith Park Boulevard and was possibly the oldest house in Hollywood. I had dug into the hillside beneath it to create a printing studio with typecases, presses, a whitewashed brick fireplace, a grand piano, and a large library. It was a hangout for the artists at Disney and others in the vicinity. Larry Powell aptly christened it "Ritchie's Road-house." Remsen Bird, then the president of Occidental College, suggested that it would be a good place to gather the many artists in the area into some sort of formal organization. The idea appealed to us and we formed what we simply called "The Club." By this time The Ward Ritchie Press had moved to a new building, so we gathered in the former quarters. Originally we met for lunch, which was "catered" by a genial old black gentle-man who had adopted us. J.D. Hicks professed to be a preacher from the Deep South, but if his preaching equalled his cooking, he was not much of a preacher. As a matter of preservation, we abandoned the luncheons and substituted evening sketch classes and as many party gatherings as our young constitutions could handle. Sketch class was regularly held every Thursday night. Landacre never missed a session, nor did J.D. until he learned that a married man could live on welfare and not work. He got married and left us. We missed his quaint ways and the slab of yellow cheese he'd hide between two slices of bread, for which we'd compensate him with a nickel. J.D. was missed, but after drawing for an hour or two, there was always a case of beer and another hour of good-natured talk.

It was an entertaining, rambunctious, and talented group that I remember well. In addition to Landacre, there were Gordon Newell, sculptor; Theodore Criley, architect; Onestus Uzzell, painter; Archibald Garner, sculptor; Jake Zeitlin, poet and bookseller; Lee Blair, artist; George Stanley, sculptor; Tee Hee, Disney artist; Merle Armitage, designer; Fletcher Martin, painter; Barse Miller, painter; Tom Craig, watercolorist; Leigh Harline, Disney composer; Grant Dahlstrom, printer; Alexander Brooks, painter; the Smith brothers, Maxson and Roger, notable lawyers; and Delmer Daves, motion picture writer and director.

Daves was the most affluent of the group, and he generously paid the monthly two dollars dues for those artists for whom it would have been a hardship. For the Saturday night parties, which we had more than occasionally, we'd assess an additional dollar that hardly covered the cost of the cheap whiskey we consumed. But "The Club" contributed more than fun and entertainment. Most of us were working on various Works Progress Administration projects, doing murals, sculptures, and designs for public buildings, schools, and post offices. One member, Merle Armitage, had been appointed regional director of the WPA, which may have been of some help to us as work on the various projects was allotted. We also helped one another. I was able to have Fletcher Martin, Barse Miller, and Landacre illustrate several books I was printing. Daves hired a carpenter to help patch the humble home of the Landacres, and the neighbors had a roofing bee to eliminate the torrent of water that poured into their house during every rainstorm. "The Club" also commissioned Paul to do a special engraving for its members. Those who could afford it paid him twenty-five dollars for a copy. "Counterpoint" was an ingenious juxtaposition of two female bodies — one of Landacre's most striking prints.

This was only a temporary stopgap to the Landacre's financial woes. To ensure a more stable income for them, Delmer Daves and Jake Zeitlin formed the Paul Landacre Association. I printed an elaborate prospectus for it, reading in part, "Realizing that none of us could individually afford to emulate the patrons of the Renaissance, and yet desiring to help an important artist to live by his work and leave him free to develop his art to a greater expression, twelve of us joined together to do as a group what we couldn't do separately."

The twelve members paid $100 a year, for which they received a new print each month. The association lasted for three years, with such diverse members as Countess Estelle Doheny, Kay Francis, Carl Zigrosser, Ruth Chatterton, Mrs. Samuel Goldwyn, and Frank Borzage. Landacre was given complete freedom to choose his subjects and to experiment as he wished. In time the pressure of originating, cutting, and printing a new block on schedule each month became too burdensome for Landacre, and the Association was allowed to expire.

Fortunately, by that time Landacre's work was getting some national recognition. His prints won several prestigious prizes and were being purchased by numerous museums and libraries, including the Museum of Modern Art, the Library of Congress, the Victoria and Albert Museum in London, and the Art Institute of Chicago, in addition to scores of West Coast institutions. Carl Zigrosser, an international authority, called him the finest engraver on the West Coast, and Rockwell Kent, at that time considered by many to be America's best, deferred to Landacre.

Book publishers were also beginning to recognize his capabilities. Donald Culross Peattie, whose *Almanac for Moderns* had been extremely popular, insisted on having Landacre illustrate several of his books, including *A Natural History of Trees of Eastern and Central North America* and *A Natural History of Western Trees*. These entailed several hundred illustrations. For a meticulous craftsman like Landacre, this was a challenge. If he had cut them in wood it might have taken him a lifetime, so he compromised and made them on scratchboard. But he insisted on drawing directly from the trees. Since this was obviously impossible, Peattie arranged for freshly cut branches from various National Parks to be sent to the Landacres. These arrived almost daily in huge boxes. Containers borrowed from neighbors were filled with water to preserve the freshness of the branches until Landacre could study and carefully sketch them. For months Paul and

Margaret enjoyed being surrounded by their own forest.

Sometime later the Limited Editions Club of New York commissioned Paul to illustrate an edition of Lucretius's *Of the Nature of Things (De Rerum Natura)*. Paul was in a dilemma. In reading the text, he couldn't find anything to illustrate. Margaret drove him over to my place where we studied the book together. My suggestion was to do some abstract illustrations with a complementing color spot. He cut a few blocks and sent proofs off to George Macy, the director of the club, for his approval. Macy was satisfied, and Paul finished the illustrations. Bruce Rogers, considered by many to have been America's finest designer of books, had been commissioned to do the layout. Rogers had never cared much for illustrators, excluding himself, intruding their concepts into books he designed, and he was not happy with Paul's illustrations. Macy was then recuperating from surgery in Beverly Hills. I visited him quite often, and on one occasion he showed me Rogers's design, which was wholly incompatible with Landacre's illustrations. Macy suggested that since I was more sympathetic to the illustrations, I should do the book. He paid Rogers his $2,000 fee and left the design and printing of the book to me.

Paul illustrated several other books for the Limited Editions Club. The last of these was Darwin's *On the Origin of the Species*, which was to be printed in Australia. It was a taxing job for which Paul did many full-page illustrations and seventy or more smaller pictures of a variety of creatures. With all of the research required, he spent more than a year on this book. It was also difficult and time-consuming to work with the printer in far-away Australia. During the progress on the book, Margaret, who had been indispensable in doing the research, began to complain of pains. Tests revealed cancer, and she died soon after.

Paul and Margaret's lives were as interwoven as any two could be. He told me that every thought, every experience that he or Margaret had, was shared. Their pleasure in simple things like going to market, Paul's day with his class at Otis Art Institute, news bits in the paper, or a magazine article were made more enjoyable by being shared and relished together. They lived for one another, and he was not prepared to live without her. Life had lost all its flavor, its joy, its color, and its hope. He said, "Without her love and presence, the pain of living isn't worth it." So he took his own life to be with her again.

Ironically, the day after his death a copy of *On the Origin of the Species,* for which they had both so eagerly waited, arrived in the mail from Australia.

# 4

## MERLE ARMITAGE
### HIS MANY LOVES AND VARIED LIVES

*Here are some intimate details not generally known of Armitage's life. He was a colorful impresario, lothario, and maverick designer. Armitage was in the forefront of those who were toppling tradition in book design during the thirties. His retinue of wives also reveals his versatility.*

I CAN'T RECALL exactly when I first met Merle Armitage. It was well over sixty years ago and probably at the bookshop of Jake Zeitlin. An interesting and creative group of young iconoclasts used to gather there to look at books and exchange ideas. Of all the frequenters, Armitage was undoubtedly the most dynamic and outspoken. He was a renegade from the East who was vocally critical of the local culture. In a talk he gave to the California Art Club on March 4, 1929, he had harsh words for his newly adopted community: "Arriving in California from New York, I was appalled by the anemic, colorless art being produced in this remote and provincial Los Angeles area. Moral, social, and sentimental values were utterly confused with aesthetic values."

This talk made a great impression on those who gathered at the bookshop, and it was decided it should be published under Zeitlin's imprint. The title of the book was *The Aristocracy of Art*.

Typographically it was brutally bold, conceived by Grace Marion Brown with help from Grant Dahlstrom and Armitage. Its bold treatment undoubtedly influenced Armitage's style when he began designing books a few years later. Its publication aroused a good deal of interest and helped start the "small renaissance" in art, letters, and printing that developed, incredibly, in southern California during the Depression years of the 1930s.

Most of Armitage's activities and accomplishments have been recorded in two autobiographies and in books by his friends. What I remember are the more intimate aspects of his life and our long years of friendship.

He was an able and driving man, full of enthusiasm and energy. He was continually delving into and promoting a variety of activities. He was raised in the Midwest and had little formal education, but having an inquiring mind and a rambling curiosity, he absorbed an incredible knowledge of music, art, and literature. His friendships eventually encompassed a who's who in the arts. While still in his teens, he migrated to New York to work with the impresario and promoter, Charles L. Wagner. With foresight and imagination, these two promoted the United States careers of many who were to become household names — John McCormack, Amelita Galli-Curci, Mary Garden, Rosa Ponselle, Feodor Chaliapin, Leopold Stokowsky, Martha Graham, Arnold Schoenberg, and Igor Stravinsky.

Armitage was accused of occasionally using unethical schemes to get newspaper publicity for his clients in the cities where they were scheduled to appear. He admitted to planting occasional fictitious gossip to keep his clients' names in the news, but denied any responsibility for an episode that salvaged a tour he was handling for a Russian opera company. The tour had begun on the West Coast with little success and was in deep financial trouble by the time it arrived in Chicago. Armitage had to borrow from several friends just to pay the railroad fare to get the troupe there after a disastrous engagement in the South. On the opening night of the opera, *The Tsar's Bride*, there was a wild Cossack dance with eight girls doing dizzy whirling dervish dances. During this frenzy one of the dancers lost her panties and, unaware, continued to dance bare-bottomed. In those pre-enlightened days, this was scandalous news, and the papers made the most of it, resulting in oversold houses that salvaged the tour.

Merle was involved with women throughout his life — those he managed, those he lusted after, and those he married. Of those he married, none seemed to satisfy him completely, or, possibly, he them. He once wrote to me, "I must say, my life is a demonstration of the fact women have the wrong chemistry for me, loving them as I do." His first wife, from his youth, he dismissed as forgotten when I once queried him. The next was Fanchon, a spectacular woman who for many years created the Fanchon and Marco Reviews for the Paramount Theater in Los Angeles. After she divorced Merle and married actor Monte Blue, Jake Zeitlin and Merle shared an apartment for a while. Jake was continually amazed at Merle's conquests and his eclectic tastes in women, which seemed to range from floozies to socialites. According to Jake, Merle was swimming one day at the beach in Santa Monica when an extremely attractive woman swam close by. Impulsively he shouted, "Will you marry me?" Her immediate reply was, "Why not?" They swam ashore through the breakers, contemplating each other. They were soon dressed. Merle picked up his friend Jose Rodriquez, as a witness, and they drove to Tijuana for the wedding. The marriage didn't last long, and it was a fiery one.

My first exposure to Merle's penchant for the ladies was in

1932 when he was living on Orange Street in Los Angeles in a modest California bungalow. The rooms were practically bare except for the bedroom, which contained an enormous bed, long before king and emperor-size beds had become popular. It was covered with a dazzling purple spread. Innocently I asked him why he needed such a large bed. He responded that since he had two and sometimes three bedmates at once, it was more comfortable.

The first Armitage wife I knew personally was Elise. She was a tall, gangly creature who was talented and warmhearted, but not especially attractive. She had appeared in several movies with W.C. Fields. She also illustrated several of Armitage's books, and E. Weyhe published a book of her paintings. The Armitages had built a house on a hillside overlooking Silver Lake in Los Angeles, not far from where The Ward Ritchie Press was then located. It had a large living room with wall space to display a part of Merle's art collection, a single bedroom, and quantities of storage closets for an excess of paintings and clothes.

Elise was an adroit and sympathetic foil for Armitage. We often sat in the spacious front room with a generous drink in hand as she coaxed hours of delightful tales of his varied experiences from him. His life had been interwoven with so many famous people, and he recounted tales of them with great gusto and humor. As a boy he had two absorbing interests — trains and art. His mother disapproved of either as a career. She considered trains to be dangerous and was convinced that artists were destined for lives of sinful poverty. After he became successful as an impresario, she told him he could now buy pictures, which was better than having to paint them. And that he did, having some six hundred paintings, prints, and drawings displayed and stashed around his home.

He was interested chiefly in contemporary art, the works of Klee, Picasso, Kandinsky, Miro, and such. He commented, "Modern artists have given the world a rejuvenating release from old forms, old attitudes, and the dominance of literary content which even the greatest painters infused in their work." And in speaking of his collecting hobby, he added, "Nothing was a better foil or more refreshing release from the tense and capricious world of managing prima donnas, tenors, and dancers. Advances in interest and understanding produced definite plateaus of aesthetic intoxication. Art had many appeals to me, one being its spirit of freedom."

Merle and Elise were separated and divorced during World War II. He had been an enlistee in the Army during World War I, and he was eager to join again, even before the United States became involved in the new war. His preference was the Navy. He had written a book on the U.S. Navy which was highly recommended by Admiral H.S. Stark, the chief of operations. Armitage applied to him for a commission and was informed that his request would be processed immediately. Months of waiting followed. In the meantime a friend in the Air Force recommended him for a commission in that branch. He was quickly inducted as a major, and the next day he heard from the Navy that he would receive a commission of lieutenant commander, which he now couldn't accept.

He spent the early part of the war in Detroit with the Materiel Command, expediting supplies and negotiating contracts. Late in 1943 he was transferred to a pioneering project, the Air Force Redistribution Center, with headquarters in Atlantic City. Its purpose was to rehabilitate fliers who had become fatigued from long combat duty, rest them for a time in luxurious surroundings, and then reassign them to new duties where their combat experience could be used in training recruits.

In the meantime he had become attached to his comely secretary Elsa, and he married her after divorcing Elise. She bore his only child, a girl they named Chama after the beautiful Chama Valley north of Taos in New Mexico. One of the Redistribution Centers was the Miramar Hotel in Santa Monica, California. Armitage had to visit it occasionally. On one of his trips west aboard a P-24, he noticed some rock pinnacles in the desert soon after crossing the Colorado River. He was struck by the grandeur of their beauty and asked the pilot to circle around so that he could make a rough map of their location. After the war he and Elsa rediscovered the place while on a backpacking trek, filed a homesteader's claim on a choice location, and began the building of their dream house.

Early in the 1950s Merle invited my wife, Marka, and me to spend a weekend with them on their new Manzanita Ranch. It sounded quite elegant and Marka was thrilled, envisioning a few days of Palm Springs luxury, lolling in the sun by a cool pool, with gourmet meals in fancy restaurants. She bought a fetching new swimsuit and packed her finery, including a couple of décolleté evening dresses to impress the natives. Merle met us at the post office in Yucca Valley, a small town near Palm Springs, having warned us that we might otherwise have trouble finding his place. He was right. He arrived in a dust-covered Jeep and led us at high speed down the Victorville highway. Suddenly he turned off the paved road to follow barely discernible tracks through the sagebrush and cactus. I was driving a new car, one of those low-slung, slim, and sleek Studebakers with which Raymond Loewy had revolutionized postwar car design. It was not designed for dodging boulders, trampling sagebrush, and bumping through gullies, all of which were necessary to follow the dust trail of the high-hung Jeep. We managed to keep up for many tortuous miles before we finally sighted Merle's primitive paradise.

It was hardly what we had expected, though it was a place of great natural beauty with its rock pinnacle monuments, its Joshua trees, cacti, and skies of infinite blue. We came to a dusty stop and gazed around. Marka's eyes widened in disbelief. There was a structure, partially completed, with a couple of workmen on the roof. In a completely open makeshift shower, the amply-endowed Elsa was scrubbing her enticing body under a trickle of water. She waved to us and, drying off, welcomed us to the ranch. The workmen paid attention neither to the naked Elsa nor to us. I wouldn't describe Marka's immediate reaction as ecstatic. Merle produced a most appreciated drink as we unloaded our vacation gear. We carried our numerous bags and dumped them on a packing box on one side of the half-built structure. We needed another drink as we contemplated the bed on which we were to luxuriate for the next few nights. There, under the open sky, was a rusty box spring mattress with a couple of rather dirty blankets. The other accommodations were equally primitive. A hundred feet away was a hole dug in the desert with a plank straddling two boxes on which one could squat and view the lonely desert. Merle referred to his open-air privy as "The Illusion of Privacy."

In subsequent years we visited the ranch under more luxurious conditions. Merle had completed a complex of a half-dozen buildings that fitted perfectly into the desert landscape. There were now bedrooms with baths, a marvelous kitchen, a covered patio, and workshops, in addition to the original building that had been made into a library or gallery. Braques and Picassos were on the walls, and Stravinsky's chords broke through the desert silence. Merle, who had received a cordon bleu from the Wine and Food Society and who had written a couple of cookbooks, created gourmet fare for us. There were hazards, however. Rattlesnakes sometimes sallied onto the warm concrete slab of the patio, and there was an acute scarcity of water. Lacking a well on the property, Merle bought a tank truck and built a cistern up the hill to supply water, which had to be brought in from a dozen miles away. As a warning against excessive use of this scarce fluid, he had conspicuously posted many subtle signs about the property: "Please drink the Bourbon instead of the Water" or "Don't use the potty if a cactus plant is handy."

Elsa was a Midwestern farm girl with few cultural pretensions when she married Armitage. But she was apt and bright, and, in living with Merle and associating with his range of creative friends, she absorbed culture and, finally aspiring for even greater stimulation, left Merle for another. Bitter as this was to him, he wasted little time before becoming involved with Elsa's good friend Isabelle, daughter of the French novelist Lucie Heymans. Isabelle was an active, vibrant woman who had fought heroically with the French underground during the war. Eventually they were married and settled at the ranch. Lucie, and Isabelle's two children by a previous marriage came to live there.

Eventually Isabelle tired of the isolation of life on the ranch and began to fall back on her childhood religion to occupy her empty hours. She would drive the long twenty-five miles each day to attend Mass at the nearest Catholic church. Merle was concerned and did what he could to make her lot a bit happier. In 1960 I received a letter from him saying that with the children gone and Lucie spending most of her time in Paris, "we found ourselves sort of rattling around in the big place, and with all the work to keep it up. Yet we don't want to sell it. We have purchased two beautiful, juniper-covered acres in the highlands above Yucca Valley and only seven miles from the Post Office . . . and in the meantime, we are beginning to dispose of things that will not go into a smaller place."

He disposed of his extensive library through Dawson's Book Shop, and the University of Texas gave him $5,000 for files of correspondence, which delighted him as he considered them as "so much accumulated junk," though they contained letters from numerous celebrities he knew well. The new house was never built, and they moved to Santa Fe. From there he wrote, "Isabelle became increasingly absorbed in religion, to the point that no conversation, except on religious matters, was possible. This led to our removal to Santa Fe, where she could be close to the Church and Msgr. Rodriquez, her spiritual adviser. She belongs to the Altar Society, sings in choir at the Cathedral, teaches religion at St. Francis School, studies theology at St. Michaels College, teaches religion and ethics at Loretto Academy, and is now the secretary of the Santa Fe Archdiocesan Council."

It was obvious that she didn't have much time to devote to their marriage; he filled his time with writing and designing. For some reason, about which I never queried him, Merle was threatened with "a very heavy lawsuit" which caused him to transfer most of his assets, including the ranch, to Isabelle. He retained a joint bank account from which he withdrew $15,000 to send to his daughter, Chama, to cover her college expenses at Sarah Lawrence. This infuriated Isabelle, and she withdrew the balance of the account and divorced him after eleven years of marriage. She allowed him life tenancy on the ranch and the bulk of his pictures, though she took "some very rare Picassos, Paul Klees, Kandinskys, a stunning Goya, and a great Miro," Armitage wrote me. The balance he had to sell to help support himself. The sale was headlined in the *Los Angeles Times,* "Closed Circuit Art Auction Sets Records." It went on to say that the highest price paid was for a rare print by Vincent Van Gogh, but a drawing by Modigliani and lithographs by Cezanne, Gauguin,

Chagall, Matisse, and Klee also brought whopping prices.

But the story of Merle's loves proves difficult to complete. New evidence is continually brought to my attention. Quite recently, Decherd Turner, then director of the Humanities Research Center at the University of Texas, recalled that he once bought a collection of Armitage books in Guadalajara for Southern Methodist University. They were from the library of Marlende von Ruhs, who claimed that she had once been married to Armitage, and some of the inscriptions in the books bear evidence to it. Most of these books were initially inscribed to Isabelle, whose name had been scratched over with Marlende's substituted. In one copy he had written, "For darling Marlende from her lover, friend, admirer — husband." All of the books are dated 1965. Isabelle had divorced him in 1964. Merle seldom waited long between affiliations. Marlende was an artist whom I had met when she had a studio in Mendocino. The courtship had been quite one-sided. She barely knew Armitage when she began receiving from him, almost daily, long and torrid love letters, which she proudly preserved and let me read. Finally Merle came to her in person and carried her off to the mountains near Prescott, Arizona, where they self-performed an Indian marriage ceremony. The marriage lasted a bare two weeks, and Marlende said it was never actually consummated. This may have been Merle's final attempt at matrimony. What happened thereafter? Robert Purcell, in his book, *Merle Armitage Was Here*, remarks, "One day I happened to comment on seeing him with a very nice looking widow of about forty, four decades his junior. On being queried about her, he quite casually muttered, 'Oh yes. She comes out to the ranch and services me.' "

Back in 1932 the Great Depression was with us. Armitage, sitting in his office in the old Louis Sullivan–designed Philharmonic Auditorium Building in Los Angeles with few scheduled events to occupy his time, began writing about artists he'd known. He soon converted his jottings into books, and in 1932 he wrote, designed, and printed books on Warren Newcombe, Maier-Krieg, Rockwell Kent, and Richard Day. He also compiled a book of the photographs of Edward Weston. He then induced Alfred A. Knopf and E. Weyhe to publish these books.

Thus was born a maverick designer who has had a considerable influence on the appearance of the modern book. Earlier he had been responsible for printed pieces done to promote his clients' theatrical appearances and shows. His book design followed the bold and flamboyant style he had used in these pieces. He was considered by traditional designers to be an outlaw and was often criticized, but he could not have cared less. He helped liberate American book typography from convention.

During the promotion of his book on Eugene Maier-Krieg, Merle visited Maier-Krieg's studio often. On these visits, Merle would sometimes drop by my studio, which was only a few blocks away. I had just returned from my apprenticeship in Paris to start The Ward Ritchie Press in a small printing studio behind my family home in South Pasadena. Merle and I would chat and exchange ideas about the craft in which we were both comparative novices.

I have never known a man with such drive and energy. He was overflowing with ideas for books to write or compile — books on Stravinsky, Schoenberg, Martha Graham, Millard Sheets, Picasso, Paul Klee, Jean Charlot, and on and on. He reveled in his new avocation and remarked to his friend Henry Miller, "I write books so I can design them." Miller, himself a maverick, surprisingly answered, "But your books have no tradition." That is true, but they were innovative, bold in concept with great variety in content and design.

Merle was an accomplished publicist, not only for his clients but for himself. He decided that his new career needed more exposure. He wrote to me, "Coming out of a clear sky, the firm of E. Weyhe, who have published about half of the 21 books I have designed, want me to do a book on them, and have suggested a title *21 — An Adventure in Book Designing*. There will be articles by a number of critics and bookmen and I would be very pleased if you could contribute to it. As you know, my approach has been to let the punishment fit the crime or let the subject of the book dictate its design and format. I have the greatest respect for book tradition, but believe in many cases certain forms are outmoded and empty, and when they are perpetuated, they tend to draw the spirit of the book back into periods of the past which have no identification with today."

The book was published under the title *Designed Books*. In addition to my article and those of a half-dozen friends such as Carl Zigrosser, Edwin Corle, and Manuel Komroff, it contained page reproductions from each of the books Armitage had designed up to the point of the book's publication in 1938. While most of the contributions were paeans of praise, as Merle wished from his friends, I attempted to analyze the factors involved in his break with tradition and how it evolved.

Merle sent copies of the book to many influential people, including George Macy, the director of the Limited Editions Club. Macy had started the club in 1928, just before the 1929 panic. The collecting of press books was then in vogue. His plan was to issue an edition of a classic each month to 1,500 subscribers. Each edition was to be illustrated by a well-known artist and printed by one of the world's fine printers. Macy was a superb salesman in print. His announcements of forthcoming books so whetted the appetites of his subscribers that his club weathered the Depression without too many problems.

While Macy was basically a conservative bookman, the

innovative and modern designs of Armitage's books interested him. He was contemplating the production of the utopian novel *Looking Backward*, by Edward Bellamy. Since the book was supposed to have been written in the year 2000, Macy figured that he should get the most avant garde modernist he could find to design it. Armitage fit this mold perfectly, and Macy selected him to design the book. Evidently he had liked my appraisal of Armitage in *Designed Books*, and he commissioned me to print the edition.

Macy wrote of his decision in his monthly letter to subscribers, "To make a book in the taste, and with the materials of the years 1929 to 1941 would be pointless, since it bears no relation to those years. But then, on a bright day last year, a startling idea came to us. The idea was that, since Edward Bellamy made the pretense that he was writing the book in the year 2000, we might, with justification to ourselves and pleasure to our members, create an edition of the book with the pretense that it was printed in the year 2000. The idea came to us while we were laboring under what the psychologists call a special stimulus. We had been inspecting a book called *Designed Books* by Merle Armitage . . . all of the books he makes are original, startling and fresh, and often disturbing."

We printed *Looking Backward* almost half a century ago. Today its appearance would hardly seem unusual, with its square format and illustrations in violent colors by Armitage's wife at the time, Elise, but it got heated reactions then. Macy may have anticipated repercussions from his members, as he wrote to them when the book was sent, "This is an unusual book. If you like it, as we think you will, or if you don't like it at all, as we think you won't, we hope you will write to us to give us your opinion, so we can send word out to Hollywood, to tell that bull-in-our-china-shop, that man Merle Armitage, what effect his dynamic ideas have upon ultra-conservatives like you and like us."

He could hardly have been prepared, however, for his members' reactions, as he reported in the next issue of his monthly letter: "We don't know at this moment how many letters we have received in comment upon that book. We haven't the courage to count them. Here and there among them, we come upon a letter of praise. But the letters of abuse of the book pile higher and higher in the files; and, when the kind of literate person who is a member of this Club wants to be abusive, he knows how to be abusive." He quotes from several of the letters, ending with one from a gentleman in Florida who wrote, "*Looking Backward* is the lousiest book, in my opinion, you have ever published." Not everyone was that critical. Paul McPharlin, a distinguished book designer from Michigan, wrote Macy, "*Looking Backward,* done for you by Merle Armitage, is one of the most luxurious of his characteristic books."

Edward Weston was among Armitage's close friends, and one of the first books Armitage did was a superb book of Weston photographs printed for him by Lynton Kistler. It was handsome enough to be selected as one of the Fifty Books of the Year by the American Institute of Graphic Arts. The adverse criticism of *Looking Backward* hardly fazed Armitage. He continued to besiege Macy with suggestions for other books he'd have liked to design for the club. Macy was not interested in again afflicting his members with Armitage. He turned down proposals for *Carmen* and *Death Comes for the Archbishop.* But when Merle suggested *Leaves of Grass* with photographic illustrations by Edward Weston, he got a positive response.

Weston was not destitute, but he was hardly affluent. With an advance from Macy, he was able to get a new car and spend months in Whitman country taking pictures to illustrate the poems. It was arranged that Armitage would design the book and I would print it. Weston completed his assignment to everyone's satisfaction. But then the fireworks began in a contest between two willful and opinionated men, with me in the middle receiving a barrage of recriminating letters from each as they fought their minor war.

Macy, with his usual exuberant flair, wrote a glowing preview of the book in his prospectus for the season of 1942. Merle had in the meantime been inducted into the Air Force. He sent me rough layouts and instructions from Detroit, and I made up a dummy with sample pages which he submitted to Macy. On April 10, 1942, a letter came to Major Armitage, War Department, Air Corps, Materiel Division, Detroit, Michigan, as follows: "Dear Merle: You will have already heard the good news, that Edward Weston has completed the illustrations for *Leaves of Grass* and has sent me a set of proofs. I have wired him, and written him, to tell him that I am overjoyed; they are wonderful photographs, and they do the job of illustration wonderfully well. I am proud of him for having made the photographs, and proud of myself for having thought of the idea. Until now, all of us have been taking it for granted that you would design the book and Ward Ritchie would print it. Therefore, I earnestly hope you will not grow apoplectic when I tell you that I would like to change this plan. As you know, I was not happy over the dummy you prepared, although I was unable to express my unhappiness in words. But now I want to have your permission to turnabout and give this job to Kittredge at The Lakeside Press in Chicago. As I look over the photographs, I get the feeling that he is the man to make the kind of job which I would like to have. Possibly you will not grow apoplectic at all, you may be so busy with your work in Detroit that you cannot possibly undertake to produce this book for us; you may even have been wondering how you could let me down. If this is so, I will be greatly relieved. If you have been planning on designing the book, and will now conclude that I am letting you down, I will be very sorry."

This letter infuriated Major Armitage, especially because Macy took credit for suggesting Weston. He replied three days later, "Dear George: It was my suggestion that you do a book with Edward Weston's photographs. I have a written agreement with you to design *Leaves of Grass* with photographs by Edward Weston. That fact has been advertised. At your written suggestion, I proceeded with the designs. My work in furthering this enterprise, including considerable personal effort and expense — as well as my achievements as a designer — are involved. I cannot and will not accept the implications of your letter of April 10."

Many acrimonious letters from each followed. Armitage wrote, "You would have to satisfy me there was a designer available who could be trusted to achieve that certain contemporary yet universal feeling in the format and design of the book which would be proper and authoritative. After all, the man who designs this book must appropriately set the stage for two tremendous men, Whitman and Weston. Further, you would have to compensate me in some manner for the fact that you have advertised me as the only man in America to design a book of photographs (or words to that effect), in announcing this *Leaves of Grass* edition. I don't think it is probable that you will satisfy me either as to another designer or as to compensating for the announcement."

In reply Macy wrote, "The letter you sent me on April 22 is the damn foolest letter I have received in my life." He went on to say, "I have greatly admired some of the books you have planned in the past, although I have considered others of your books showed little taste or sense. . . . When you sent me the first trial for *Leaves of Grass*, I thought it very bad, but I told you only that there were some things I didn't like about it. . . . I now regret infinitely those hypocrisies on my part."

A few days later I had a letter from Merle, "It looks like we have won our battle with Macy. I received a letter from him today, cursing me wildly, but giving me three alternatives, one of which is for us to go ahead as we originally planned. Now it is our turn to laugh."

He was premature; Macy had the final laugh. Macy designed the format himself and had the book printed by the Aldus Printers in New York. But Armitage was not to be left without some last words, which he sent to Macy after seeing a copy of the finished book, "My dear George: I took *Leaves of Grass* home last night and have changed my mind in regard to my comments, as I think, in justice to you, something should be said. You have succeeded magnificently in turning out the world's most deluxe 'Grass Seed Catalog.' "

Merle and Elsa returned to California after the war and spent a relaxing vacation trudging through the Sierra and down through the desert as far as Santa Fe. In 1947 Merle received a letter from Gardner Cowles, the publisher of *Look* magazine, saying he'd like to discuss the appearance of the magazine with him. Cowles was impressed by the design of Armitage's books and, realizing that the appearance of his magazine was about the shoddiest on the market, hoped that this man might be able to improve its appearance and make it more competitive with *Life*. They met for lunch at the Beverly Hills Hotel, and Merle's criticism of the magazine's format sufficiently impressed Cowles that he suggested Merle take a trip to New York to meet the *Look* staff. Merle conferred with several local typographers and had several experimental pages set before going East. In the meantime Cowles had fired his art director to replace him with Armitage, much to Merle's surprise. He was uncomfortable at first in his new job, as there was considerable resentment over his abrupt appointment. He was aggressive and outspoken, but his past experience in show business had familiarized him with the art of pleasing people; he soon had a content and cooperative group. His show business experience also helped him change the appearance of the magazine to appeal more to the general public. In addition to being the art director, he was made a member of the editorial board and later chairman. Here he exerted a great deal of effort to harmonize the contents of the magazine with its new format.

Though he was not completely responsible, the fact remains that during the six years he was with *Look* its circulation rose from 2 million copies to over 5 million copies per issue. He also trained his staff well, which allowed him to spend considerable time in outside activities. He was active in the American Institute of Graphic Arts, serving as president for a term, and he designed books for several New York publishers. Also Cowles discovered what a persuasive and articulate speaker he was and sent him to conferences and conventions to address agencies on the advantages of advertising in *Look*. He once estimated that he made more than 100 speeches during his association with the magazine.

Characteristic of his many talks was the one given at the convention of the American Association of Advertising Agencies, where he said in part, "What is the Grammar of Design? We know very little about this. From the adoption of perspective in painting to today's preoccupation with flat pattern, we have sensed many things and discovered a few. But the basic power is not fully revealed. We know that a cross is a static symbol. We know that red is an exciting color, possibly because it is the color of blood. We know that blue contains a message of distance, possibly because it is the color of the infinite sky. We know that a flat line, such as the horizon at sea, is restful and optimistic, possibly because when we were infants we did not fall off a flat surface. We know that the down-sweep of a bird is laden with a certain excitement, because it is related to an eventual recovery, or a regained flight. We know a few of the basic laws. But can we put a page together that can arrest people, convince people, and cause people to act in our favor?"

It is obvious that Merle's six years in New York were typical of his aggressive activity. In addition to his work with *Look*, he was instrumental in the publication of a new magazine called *Quick*. He was an editor of and a contributor to *Books in our Time*, and he was one of a distinguished group of designers included among the speakers at a four-day forum sponsored by The Book-builders Workshop and the Harvard University Press. Some of Armitage's comments at that forum in 1949, published in *Basic Forms* by the Harvard University Press, show some of his conception of the present and future status of the book.

Here are some of his statements, taken out of context, which indicate some of his beliefs: "The printing of today will not reach new horizons by looking backward. . . . Looking backward means forsaking adventure, experimentation, research, and the opportunity to make new and significant statements allied to our particular times. . . . Backward looking is a basic menace to growth. . . . The world is about to enter upon one of the most gigantic battles of modern times . . . our whole economy will tremble and writhe and expand to meet the changes this new concept of manufacturing will certainly bring. . . . The book, as we know it, has lost its direction, its leadership . . . it has been left far behind in this time of technological changes . . . it seems singularly unaware of today's problems."

In 1953 Armitage returned to California with sufficient severance funds to complete his dream complex on his desert ranch. While he was nominally retired, he was never inactive. His interests were wide-ranging. He continued to design books. He never lost interest in trains and wrote two books on the Santa Fe and another entitled *Railroads of America*. He published books under the imprint of the Manzanita Press. He was fascinated by native American art. On a visit to the Laboratory of Anthropology in Santa Fe, he happened to pick up a dull-appearing book, only to find that the color reproductions inside were fantastic. He mentioned his discovery to the director, who told Merle that the book just didn't sell. Merle suggested that if the Laboratory would allot him a couple of hundred dollars, he'd guarantee to make it do so. It was agreed, and after Merle designed a colorful wrapper of Indian symbols to hide the drab cover, the book began to sell briskly. As a result he was asked to design many subsequent books for the laboratory. In the last few years of his life, he began a new career as an artist, creating collages of Indian designs.

Though we corresponded, I hadn't seen Merle for several years when he arrived unexpectedly one day at my Laguna Beach home, accompanied by his sculptor friend, Maier-Krieg. This was early in March of 1975. He had gained a lot of weight, some fifty pounds since I had last seen him. He was in good spirits, full, as always, of his robust tales and proud of being so healthy at the age of eighty-two.

It wasn't more than a week before I received a phone call that he had suffered a massive stroke. I was told that even as he lay paralyzed and unable to speak, his eyes smiled as he completed his abundant life.

# 5

## ROBINSON JEFFERS
### RECOLLECTIONS OF THE POET

*Robinson Jeffers is undoubtedly California's finest poet. Ritchie
became interested in his poetry while still in college, and when he began
to print, one of his first books was Robinson Jeffers' Stars. There has
been a lengthy relationship between the two, resulting in Ritchie
being involved in more than a dozen of Jeffers' books.*

WHERE THE SEA is its most restless on the rugged coast of California, from Monterey to beyond Big Sur, is the part of the world that Robinson Jeffers loved and about which he wrote. The tower of stone and the house he built in Carmel for his wife, Una, stands there, no more surrounded by the hundreds of trees he planted to protect his privacy.

I recall the year 1928 when I read his *Roan Stallion, Tamar and Other Poems.* This experience seems to have had a touch of destiny about it, as I realize the extent to which the writing of Jeffers has been woven into the pattern of my own life's work. At Occidental College, my friend Gordon Newell had bought a book as a present for a girl he liked. He thought he was getting a volume by Edwin Arlington Robinson, but instead he had purchased a Robinson Jeffers' book. After glancing through the poem *Tamar,* he had immediate misgivings as to its appropriateness for his innocent girlfriend. Because he had written in it and couldn't return it, he gave the book to me.

Almost sixty years have passed, but as I now look at this copy of *Roan Stallion*, I can see how it captivated me at that time. I had underlined it and annotated it with such comments as "Impermanent beauties are not poetry's stuff," and "The beauty of emergence into black nothingness surpasses the religious promises of life after death." This book initiated an interest in Jeffers not only for me but also for Gordon Newell and Lawrence Clark Powell. The three of us began to saturate ourselves with Jeffers' poems. We also interested Occidental College president Remsen Bird in the poet, who had graduated from the college in 1905. Previously the circulation of Jeffers' books in the Occidental College library had been restricted to graduate students, but soon, rather than being suppressed in embarrassment, they were circulated with pride.

In 1929, after floundering in and out of law school in search of a career, I settled on printing. In trying to teach myself this craft, I wrote to poets I admired for permission to print some of their poems in a series of small booklets. Most of them graciously allowed me to do so. Carl Sandburg, Léonie Adams, Archibald MacLeish, Hildegarde Flanner, Louise Bogan, and, of course, Robinson Jeffers all allowed me to print their work. Jeffers suggested two sonnets which had previously appeared in *The Bookman*.

In 1930, while working in the *atelier* of François-Louis Schmied, I printed a group of Jeffers' poems entitled *Apology for Bad Dreams* in my spare time. On my way back to California in 1931, I stopped in New York to see the printers and sights of that city. Among them was Elmer Adler's press, the Pynson Printers. It was a model small plant dedicated to the making of beautiful books. As we sat in Adler's library talking about printing, I showed him my *Apology for Bad Dreams*. He then told me that he had been imploring Jeffers to write an article on the publication of his first book for *The Colophon*, a luxurious bibliographic quarterly which Adler edited and published. He said that his entreaties had thus far been unsuccessful, and he hoped that if and when I saw Jeffers I might be able to persuade him to write something.

During the years since college, Gordon Newell had served an apprenticeship in sculpture with Ralph Stackpole in San Francisco and had then moved with his wife, Gloria Stuart, to Carmel, where he was captivated by the spell of that beautiful area and Jeffers' modeling of its mood and grandeur. He wrote me in 1930, while I was still in Paris: "They [the Jeffers] are great admirers of the four Powys brothers, John Cowper in particular. A sister of the Powys is a convert of Jeffers and corresponds regularly. Llewellyn P., when he read *Tamar*, exclaimed, 'With Jeffers' courage and what I know about incest and perversion, what couldn't I have done with that story!' Jeffers admires Maurice Maeterlinck and George Moore. The new room is now roofed [Newell was speaking of the addition to Jeffers' house] and I am doing some carving for it of a minor nature, and some furniture. The boys are coming to me for instruction in carving and tool sharpening."

Lawrence Powell was also well into this Jeffers circle. The subject for his thesis at the university at Dijon was Robinson Jeffers, and he devoted the next couple of years to studying his poetry.

Not long after I returned to California, I drove up north where I picked up some type from the Grabhorns and some English paper from Hazel Dreis, the bookbinder. I also stopped off in Carmel to see the Newells and there, for the first time, met Robinson and Una Jeffers. In my notebook for Tuesday, January 5, 1932, I wrote of this meeting: "Arrived last night in Carmel to stay with Gordon and his wife Gloria. This morning had a good talk with Orrick Johns and John Catlin. Gave interview to Gloria for *The Carmelite.* About 4:30 P.M. Gordon, Gloria, and I went down to the Jeffers'. We drove up to the tree-crowded yard and parked. There was a wide gate to the inner yard and a sign proclaiming, 'Not at home until 4 P.M.' Jeffers had his day charted for writing in the morning and laboring on the house in the afternoon. There was the sound of chopping in the stone enclosure by what was possibly the kitchen door. We went to the front door and knocked. I looked over at the Hawk Tower. The door was open. The ground floor seemed to be used as a carpentry shop. Over the door was a carved standing unicorn. And then one of the sons came to the front door. He recognized the Newells, and upon being asked if his mother was at home, he very shyly answered that he would see. He returned in a short while to tell us she was and to invite us in. The room where we sat occupies the whole south side of the house, with great windows looking straight out over the ocean and others looking south across the Carmel River to Point Lobos. A fireplace is in the middle of the north side, and doors on either side lead to other parts of the house. Back on the inside east is a built-in bench — and on the sides are bookcases, with other bookcases built around the room. There are quantities of books, a grand piano, and a lovely highboy on which is a big clock and a table with a carbon lamp. There is no electricity. I looked at the books on the shelf near to where I sat. There were a couple of short rows of books on Byron, many on Shelley, the Brontes, etc.

"Mrs. Jeffers entered through one of the doors by the fireplace. She is short and slightly plump. Her hair is long and braided in two strands down her back to below her hips. It is slightly streaked with gray. She was rather untidily dressed, but her greeting was full of enthusiasm, and as soon as we were introduced she said, 'I'll run and tell Robin.' She returned and he followed soon afterwards. He came over and we shook hands. He eyed me furtively. Then we were all seated — he on the bench at the back of the room. He seemed very human and even jovial and talkative. He cracked a couple of jokes and talked a bit of his European experiences. He entered into the spirit of the group completely, often with happy, open smiles.

"We talked of *Descent to the Dead*, which had just been published. The publishers had sent him only three copies. They had also sent him a limited edition of the Nonesuch *Donne*, which Una showed us with much pride. They also had several other Nonesuch books — and in fact seemed to keep up on modern books (there was even a newspaper scattered in one corner of the room). Una suggested to Robin that he pour some wine, and we all drank some very good homemade wine. His face is kindly, with deep lines, and not hard and stonelike as I had expected. He wore breeches, old leather leggings, and older shoes. He was in true working clothes.

"He told of the great storm of last week and how it had brought one huge boulder over the road, which was too great for him to move in the wheelbarrow. He said nowhere south is there vigor such as there is here — 'though Laguna had been nice, and Palos Verdes, before the influx of people.' The Hershbeins had been up. Una said they were people she'd like to cultivate if she only had time. Jeffers told of one of the picturesque scenes in India they had described, where the great flocks of eagles would fly up at sunset, higher and higher into the sky to get the last glimpse of the setting sun. They told about having stopped at Kelmscott Manor in England and seeing the William Morris home and the Kelmscott *Chaucer* laid out on the bed.

"Una asked Robin to build us a fire, and very slowly and gracefully he moved about to do it. When he sat in the corner, first smoking his pipe and later a cigarette, he seemed the essence of contentment and perfect repose listening to our chatter.

"I mentioned the article Elmer Adler had asked him to write for *The Colophon*. Una said that Albert Bender had just written, urging him to do it, and had sent down a copy so they could see what it was like. Jeffers said he had read the similar article by Hugh Walpole and was sure he couldn't write anything as long or as interesting. Una seemed to think it might be a nice gesture, but they only paid fifty dollars for an article.

"We spoke of Powell and they said they had a letter of his unopened. Jeffers said he hadn't read it yet as it looked to be long and complicated. He said that Powell wrote very interestingly. Una said that she had left it for Robin to answer. She got it out and opened it. It proved to be a review of some of Jeffers' work by a Sorbonne professor, which Powell had translated.

"I told him about a publishing project I was planning and asked if he could contribute something. He said he didn't know, he'd have to think it over. It was always difficult for him to get anything together, even for his publisher.

"I asked him about *Flagons and Apples.* He said there had been 500 copies printed just a short time before he had gone to Seattle. He had taken a half dozen or so with him and had left the rest with the printer. Sometime later the printer wrote and asked what he should do with the balance of the books. Jeffers told him to destroy them as wastepaper. Apparently the printer couldn't bear to do that. They eventually turned up in Holmes Bookstore where the printer had evidently remaindered them. There were also 500 copies of the Peter Boyle edition of *Tamar and Other Poems* printed, for which Jeffers had paid.

"It was six o'clock. When we were getting ready to leave, I asked Jeffers if he would autograph my collection of his books. I brought the whole stack in, which I had left in the car. He was interested in the first Boni-Liveright announcement of which I had a copy. He recalled having seen it, though Una never had. He said it probably contained the first appearance of his auto-biographical sketch. I left the books and said I'd come back for them on Saturday. He said that would be fine as it would give him plenty of time. Una asked what I wished written in them as she would have to see that it was done.

"We left, shaking hands again. He said he was glad to have met me at last, and Una said that we'd probably correspond now.

"That night Orrick Johns, Gordon, Gloria, and I had a gallon of red wine and a flowing of talk. Orrick was wonderful. He told us that he had discovered Jeffers' poetry when he (Johns) was living in Italy and immediately wrote Jeffers, 'Now that I have read *Tamar* I no longer have to apologize for American poetry.' Jeffers replied and told how *Roan Stallion* was based on a story he'd heard of a woman in Turin who had erected a statue there to a horse that had been her lover. Orrick considered *Roan Stallion* and *The Loving Shepherdess* to be the best of the longer poems, and Jeffers' latest book, *Descent to the Dead*, the ultimate of what Jeffers could do with his shorter poems. He said that in the two years he had been in Carmel, Jeffers had changed from a frigidly shy and reserved man into a fairly friendly and affable fellow. He seemed to think Jeffers' best work had been written and that he could now relax and enjoy himself."

On returning to Los Angeles I unearthed a few more bits about *Flagons and Apples* and relayed them to Jeffers, hoping that he might write his story for *The Colophon*, which he promptly did. At that time I had a Washington handpress; a case of four-teen-point Garamont type, which I kept under my bed; and a smattering of well-used Eve type, which I had brought from the Grabhorns on my visit north. Assuming that I had had some responsibility for Jeffers' somewhat reluctant contribution of his article on the publication of his first book, Adler sent me a typed copy saying that he planned to have it printed on the West Coast inasmuch as this was Jeffers' locale. Each article in *The Colophon* was then designed and printed by a different printer chosen by Adler from those he considered to be the best and most suited for the particular article. *The Colophon* thus was not only of bibliographic interest but was also a typographical showcase of the work of the foremost printers of Europe and America. Adler had not as yet chosen a printer, and it was presumptuous of me, hardly more than an apprentice, to think that I could join the array of the great printers who had contributed to *The Colophon*, but I stayed up all that night and finished setting the article in my Garamont type the next morning. I called Paul Landacre and asked him if he'd be willing to do a wood engraving for me of Jeffers' Hawk Tower. With his agreement, I sketched a rough illustration on my proofs and sent them off to Adler. He couldn't have been more surprised, but he evidently liked what I had done and wrote to ask me what equipment I had. I could hardly tell him that the only press I owned was a Washington handpress on which it would have been impossible to have printed the 1,500 copies he needed in any reasonable time. I wrote him that I had a Colt's Armory press, which I had seen the Grabhorns use so effectively.

The job became mine, and The Ward Ritchie Press came into instant existence in the early part of 1932, during the very depths of the Great Depression. I scurried around and found an old Gally Universal press, which was comparable mechanically to the Colt's Armory, and started printing my first job. It was Jeffers' essay "First Book," and it appeared as the initial article in *The Colophon*, Part Ten.

Powell, meanwhile, had been working on his doctoral thesis at the University of Dijon. His thesis was printed under the title *An Introduction to Robinson Jeffers* in 1932 by Bernigaud and Privat in Dijon. Jake Zeitlin's bookshop bought the thirty or forty extra copies Powell had had printed and sold them immediately to avid Jeffers collectors. Zeitlin, in addition to his bookshop, had a small publishing venture, the Primavera Press, in which I was also involved. Upon Powell's return home to California, he worked for Zeitlin for a couple of years, during which time we induced him to revise his thesis for less scholarly publication. Rockwell Kent agreed to do a couple of illustrations and a series of initial letters, and Jeffers wrote a modest introduction, saying, "When Powell was here lately, on his return from France, my good impressions of him were excellently confirmed. We took him for a drive 'down the coast,' as we say here, to look at the scenery of the verses he had written about; but then we were astonished, though used to gray skies here, at the thickness and obstinacy of the fog that curled about the car all the way southward. Nothing could be seen, mountains nor sea nor shore. I heard Powell and my wife conversing gently in the white smother. She said, 'Robin isn't the sort of person you expected.' 'Quieter,' he answered cautiously. She said, 'You were wondering about those themes of his; did you ever think that perhaps they are chosen simply because they are interesting to him. No doubt there are psychological reasons. . . .' "

Powell's book was printed by a commercial printer, and it did not quite fulfill our expectations. While I designed it, I often regret that I wasn't allowed to print it on handmade paper as it deserved. However, Powell was pleased to have it published and wrote as an inscription in my copy: "Well, Richman, you and I have followed the trail of Robinson Jeffers together quite a few years. First of all, you bought Roan Stallion and gave it to me to read. And then in 1930, at Clyde Browne's, you printed a wretched first edition of Stars with four misspellings in one sonnet. And then we shipped out to Europe — you, 'Peter Quince,' wrote verses; and I, 'Jo Goose,' wrote a 'novel' — and I went to Dijon to write a thesis on Jeffers, and you stayed in Paris and printed his *Apology for Bad Dreams*, chez Schmied — and finally, after much wandering and much travail, we brought our own efforts together, still on the trail of Jeffers; and brought forth this slim book. And now if I didn't feel that we could do a damn sight better as we hew the path together, I would go out and fold myself.

> Yours ever,
>
> (to the elite) Lawrence Clark Powell
> (to the vulgar) Larry
> (to the pack) Jo Goose"

In 1935, which was the thirtieth anniversary of Jeffers' graduation from Occidental College, President Remsen Bird suggested a commemorative exhibition now that the college had finally come to condone Jeffers' poetry. Powell wrote and I printed a catalog, with introductions by Bird and Jeffers. Paul Landacre illustrated it with a wood engraving of the Carmel hills and several decorations. This was the first of the recognitions Occidental was to give to Robinson Jeffers.

In 1937 he was presented an honorary degree of Doctor of Literature. It was on June 7, a Monday, and I made the following notes about the occasion: "Went to the graduation ceremonies at Oxy with Larry P. We arrived late and climbed up the hill to the top of the Greek Theater where we sat looking down on the whole procedure. It was a lovely sight, with the trees grown so big — a far cry from the theater as we first knew it in 1925. Jeffers was given a Litt. D. and afterwards we went down the hill to Dr. Bird's house for a buffet supper. Gordon had arrived. Una and the two boys were there, as were Albert Bender, Dr. Judy of Caltech, Mrs. Roy Pinkham, and both the Zeitlins. Jeffers seemed quite pleased and remarked to Larry, who asked him if he had seen the exhibit of his books at Berkeley, that he had gone to see it but had balked at the door, but after today's experience could probably go any place. Tonight was the first time any of us had seen him in a suit — he is always in leggings. The talk was mostly of D.H. Lawrence, Taos, and Ireland. Una is learning Gaelic from the phonograph. Afterwards we went over to the library to see the Bender Collection of Jeffers' books, but as the lights couldn't be turned on, we peered by match light."

The sculptured head of Jeffers, which is now in the Occidental College Library, resulted from a casual remark made that night. On Wednesday, June 9, 1937, I wrote: "Yesterday afternoon Archie Garner and I went out to Mrs. Pinkham's for Archie to do a head of Jeffers. The night before I had suggested it and, getting permission, came home to tell Archie. He startedearly and molded a rough head in clay from photographs. At 4:30 we went to the Pinkham's on Sunset Boulevard, and Jeffers posed for about an hour and a half. Una commented that Archie was making Jeffers' nostrils too sensitive, whereupon Jeffers made them quiver and Una fell upon him with laughter and affection. Una talked interestingly all of the time while Jeffers sat very quietly posing, only asking for an occasional respite to roll a cigarette and relax." Regretfully Jeffers wasn't too pleased with the result, much preferring the Jo Davidson bust made several years earlier. While the Garner piece has a place of honor in the Occidental Library, Jeffers hid his copy in a dark corner of a closet in the new wing of Tor House, where it still is.

William van Wyck, a lusty and prolific writer whom I had first met in Paris and who subsequently wrote several books that The Ward Ritchie Press published, was a great admirer of Jeffers. In 1938 he sent me a short essay he had written about Jeffers. It was hardly long enough to make a legitimate book, but I liked it and decided to publish it. In order to bulk it out to at least sixteen pages, I had to pad it with some ingenious typographical designs by Alvin Lustig, who was working with me at the time. Lustig was just at the beginning of his brilliant and all-too-short career. He worked in the corner of my office with a few cases of geometrical type ornaments with which he created incredible design patterns. This was his first essay in book decoration and, following my rather silly instructions to build a flow of decorations from page to page like a symphony, he helped me make a uniquely warm and curious little book.

The Ward Ritchie Press collaborated with another artist many years later in 1956. Merle Armitage brought us a commission to print a limited edition of Jeffers' *The Loving Shepherdess* which he would design. The book was set by hand in sixteen-point Bembo type and printed on imported paper in folio size. It contained many original etchings engraved and printed by Jean Kellogg, who was a neighbor of the Jeffers in Carmel. It combined the talents of a diverse group.

In writing of Jeffers I must also include Una. She was a warm and wonderful woman, beautiful in her youth when Jeffers first met her as a student at the University of Southern California. She was Robin's contact with the world. It was she who handled the correspondence and supplied him with local lore. Before her marriage to Jeffers she had been the wife of Edward Kuster, and it was Kuster's second wife, Edith, later Mrs. James Greenan, who brought me the manuscript *Of Una Jeffers* to publish. Soon after Edith's marriage to Kuster, he had taken her to meet Una. She wrote, "Meeting your husband's *first* wife is far more difficult than meeting his mother. It becomes an emotional, feminine crisis. If Adam and Eve had had to face such undercurrents, the human race might have ended then and there."

But this seventeen-year-old girl was transfixed by Una's appearance as she saw her for that first time. And every detail remained clear in her memory when she wrote so many years later, "She made a lovely picture wearing a black velvet gown — empire style — which she herself had designed. Her dark brown hair with red glints in it was bound around her head, making her look more than ever, with her heart-shaped face, like a Botticelli Madonna.

"And Una's skin! Unbelievably white, translucent, the texture of jasmine petals. Even her jewelry reflected her individuality. A curious necklace of amber, exquisitely cut. A medieval gold ring and bracelet set with enormous topazes. A delicate faraway fragrance clung to her. She told me it was sandalwood and that she had never used anything else. I think Una is fond of sandalwood in a mystical sense. It links her with the past, with another very old world in which she feels at home. Robin loves it too, and always says by this fragrance he could recognize Una even in hell."

This book we published in 1939, and years later in 1954, after Una's death, we issued a book she had written herself entitled *Visits to Ireland, Travel-Diaries of Una Jeffers*. It is a book of which I am very fond. Paul Landacre cut a fine wood engraving of an Irish tower and Jeffers wrote a tender introduction, in which his admiration of and loving dependence upon his wife is gracefully acknowledged in beautiful and simple prose.

In 1948 Remsen Bird called my attention to another prose piece by Jeffers. It had appeared in the magazine section of the *New York Times*, and, with permission from the paper and Jeffers, we made a colorful little book out of it, handset by Caroline Anderson and Albert Yarrish. I enjoyed playfully decorating it with colorful rules and type ornaments. Its title was *Poetry, Gongorism, and a Thousand Years*, and in it Jeffers relates his theory of poetry: "I write verses myself, but I have no sympathy with the notion that the world owes a duty to poetry, or any other art.

Poetry is not a civilizer, rather the reverse, for great poetry appeals to the most primitive instincts. It is not necessarily a moralizer; it does not necessarily improve one's character; it does not even teach good manners. It is a beautiful work of nature, like an eagle or a high sunrise. You owe it no duty. If you like it, listen to it; if not, let it alone." He continues to tell us that the poet must not be distracted by the present; his business is with the future — "For thus his work will be sifted of what is transient and crumbling, the chaff of time and the stuff that requires footnotes. Permanent things, or things forever renewed, like the grass and human passions, are the material of poetry; and whoever speaks across the gap of a thousand years will understand that he has to speak of permanent things, and rather clearly too, or who would hear him?"

Jeffers had few intimate friends, though Una was quite gregarious. Among the closest to both were Theodore and Frances Lilienthal, and Melba Bennett. Lilienthal had a bookstore in San Francisco in the late 1920s and published an occasional book. He became interested in Jeffers' poetry after the publication and critical acclaim of *Tamar and Other Poems* and wrote Jeffers to ask if he would allow the publication of a strictly limited edition of some unpublished work. Jeffers made excuses at the time, but eventually did write a slight prose piece, *All the Corn in One Barn,* for the Gelber and Lilienthal bookshop in 1926. In responding to Lilienthal he mentioned, "I'd be very glad to receive a visit from you if you ever happen to be in the neighborhood."

The Lilienthals hardly paused before making this visit and many more, as Jeffers' traditional reserve thawed and a warm and continuing friendship resulted. In addition to the books published in his bookshop, Lilienthal enjoyed producing small, privately printed items which he'd give to privileged friends.

Many of these were printed for him by the Grabhorn Press, and others in even more limited quantities by his own private press, The Quercus Press, which was operated by his wife and a neighbor, Edith Van Antwerp. Jeffers cooperated and furnished many of his unpublished poems for them to print. Only a handful of each book was printed as "the little old ladies" tired after a dozen or so copies.

Jeffers relished his friendship with the Lilienthals and on Ted's sixtieth birthday wrote a poem and a touching tribute to him: "Dear Ted: Your wife telephones and gives me some family gossip: that you will attain the robust age of sixty on February twenty-fifth. From my height of sixty-six I am not impressed. But no doubt, it marks an era, and your friends have thought a poem of mine, printed by Ed Grabhorn, who is probably the best printer in the world, might be a birthday gift from them to you. I am glad to dedicate to you the poem that follows. It has just today been finished, and seems to be the best that I have written lately. The Latin title is stolen from Lucretius, as you will recognize, but I suppose 'De Rerum Natura' has become 'public domain' by this time. I will trespass again on 'public domain' in wishing you from my heart many happy returns of the day."

Upon Jeffers' death Lilienthal planned a memorial keepsake to be printed by the Grabhorns. He asked Judith Anderson, Melba Berry Bennett, Remsen Du Bois Bird, John W. Caughey, Frederick M. Clapp, Arthur G. Coons, William Turner Levy, Lawrence Clark Powell, and me to join in writing tributes. I remembered too much and filled a dozen pages which I sent to Lilienthal. He wrote back on June 4, 1962, "Your tribute to R.J. on hand, and it is excellent. But we are compressing the volume into 5,000 words and the maximum, divided into ten individual tributes, of not more than 500 words." I managed to write a shorter piece for him and gave the original to Occidental College, where it was published in the faculty-alumni magazine, *Impromptu*, in 1963. I have resurrected it and expanded it somewhat for this printing.

Melba Berry Bennett came into the Jeffers' lives much later than did the Lilienthals. As an undergraduate student at Stanford University, she had become interested in poetry and especially in the work of Jeffers. As part of her schoolwork she wrote an essay about Jeffers and the sea, which she took to Lilienthal, hoping he would be willing to publish it. He insisted she first check with Jeffers to verify some of her biographical accounts. This was in 1934, and the first meeting was not too amicable, especially with Una Jeffers, as Melba began querying Jeffers about the identity of some of the women for whom he'd written some of the poems published in *Flagons and Apples*.

As Melba later wrote, "That was when I learned at first hand about Una's temper and her possessiveness. The little room shuddered with her indignation, and her eyes flashed with fury. She insisted that she was the only woman in her husband's life or poems, and I was given the very clear impression that I'd receive no cooperation whatever, ever." Melba's determination led her to further investigation and, when she proved her hypothesis, another stormy session with Una followed. Fortunately it ended amicably with both women laughing at each other's stubbornness and Irish tempers. Una cooperated from then on, and they became close friends. The manuscript was finally finished and delivered to Lilienthal, who had the Grabhorns print it for him in 1936 under the title *Robinson Jeffers and the Sea*.

By this time the relationship between Melba Bennett and the Jeffers had become close enough for them to ask Melba if she'd become Jeffers' official biographer, with the only stipulation being that she publish nothing during Jeffers' lifetime. For the next thirty years she devoted much of her spare time to accumulating and sorting scraps of knowledge about Jeffers. She traveled to Pennsylvania, where Jeffers had been born, to interview members of his family and friends for recollections of Jeffers' childhood. She talked to his college friends and to Una's friends from the days before she married Jeffers. She preserved all this incidental information for the time when she could use it. Una cooperated with lengthy letters, some 135, before her death in 1950. Una also allowed Melba to come often to Tor House and organize the mass of Jeffers' papers. After Una's death Melba took over full responsibility for them as well as the chore of answering most of the correspondence, which had previously been Una's job. She gathered Jeffers' litter and transcribed and preserved his hundreds of notes and manuscripts written "on bits and pieces of envelopes, on discarded grocery lists, on the backs of advertisements, and even on the backs of other manuscripts or typescripts."

Jeffers died at the age of seventy-five on January 15, 1962, and Melba Bennett began the long task of putting her accumulation of material into book form. When her task was complete, she submitted it to several publishers with little success and in despair came to me to see if I'd consider printing it for her. On reading it and recognizing the mass of information she'd gathered, I agreed. The book was published in 1966, and no one could have been more pleased than Melba when she received a telegram from San Francisco saying, "I have the pleasant honor to advise you your book *The Stone Mason of Tor House* has been awarded the silver medal of the Commonwealth Club of California as one of the seven best books by California authors in 1966."

Melba Bennett died in September 1968. Ted Lilienthal, Lawrence Powell, and I prepared a small memorial booklet to her in which Powell wrote, "During their lifetime and after their death, and up until the time of her own, alas, so premature, she rendered faithful and invaluable service to Robin and Una and to all who love poetry." Lilienthal died a few years later in 1972, leaving his extensive Jeffers collection to Occidental College. It was memorialized in a volume, *Theodore Lilienthal, Robinson Jeffers, and the Quercus Press,* which I wrote, and the very same year the United States Post Office honored the memory of Robinson Jeffers by issuing a commemorative stamp with his portrait, which I affixed to the title page of each copy of the booklet.

Jeffers is gone, but we still have his voice, surely for a thousand years.

# 6

## JANE GRABHORN
### ROGUISH PRINTER OF THE JUMBO PRESS

---

*Jane Grabhorn was impetuous, impertinent, and witty. She was married to one of the brothers of the preeminent Grabhorn Press of San Francisco. She attended Scripps College. While doing much of the binding for the Grabhorn Press, she carved her own niche in the Printers' Hall of Fame with the delightfully impudent creations of her own Jumbo Press and the more sedate Colt Press.*

---

SAN FRANCISCANS were quite well acquainted with fine printing and the book tradition before the Grabhorn brothers arrived in 1919. The firm of Taylor and Taylor had long been a noteworthy printing house, and John Henry Nash had made fine printing a respectable commodity to the affluent book collectors and art patrons of the city. It was to this receptive city that Edwin Grabhorn, then thirty years old, arrived with his nineteen-year-old brother, Robert. They came from Indianapolis where Ed had owned the Studio Press and Bob had learned to set type as a part-time employee while attending college.

Their press and type, which had been shipped from Indianapolis, arrived in time for them to print and distribute an announcement in January 1920 reading, "Lovers of fine printing will be interested in the opening of a printing office at 47 Kearney Street (fifth floor) in the city of San Francisco. . . . This new San Francisco office shall strive to impart more of a personal and less of a commercial air to its work."

The Book Club of California had been organized in 1912 by a group of local bibliophiles anticipating the assemblage of a fine book exhibit for the World's Fair to be held in 1915. One of its objectives was to issue a series of limited editions for its members. During the early years these books were printed by Nash or Taylor and Taylor. The upstart Grabhorn firm, interestingly enough, was commissioned to print three books for the Club in 1921, possibly because this young firm had underbid the more complacent and established firms.

While Nash's reputation was still preeminent during the 1920s, primarily due to his wealthy patrons, book collectors and printing admirers were violently divided in their loyalties between Nash and the Grabhorns, two great but dissimilar printers. Nash was a perfectionist but never too inspired or creative. The Grabhorns, on the other hand, were artists — warm, colorful, careless sometimes, but always innovative and brilliant. There was little regard or approval between these two, although when Ed was an unknown printer in Indianapolis, he had written to Haywood Hunt in San Francisco, "John Henry Nash is some printer." However, years later in his oral history for the University of California, he said, "I used to object very much to the elaborateness of Nash. I mean he used to do a fifty dollar book and take the designs from the ten cent store."

The brothers Grabhorn were also dissimilar. Ed was outgoing and gregarious. He was the person with whom visitors and clients always wished to visit and confer. He was affable and relaxed, and, with his ever-present pipe, was always willing to chat about books and prints or oriental rugs, even while feeding sheets of paper into the Colt's Armory press. He handled the presses during the early years while Bob set the type. Ed was also a collector with many varied interests — books (chiefly western Americana), primitive paintings of the Western scene, oriental rugs, furniture, and Japanese prints. There was seldom a day without several scouts bringing in treasures or pure junk for Ed to consider. He was a shrewd and prolific buyer. As a result the printshop became a museum cluttered with Ed's purchases.

Bob was more of an intellectual, though it was never apparent. Quiet and reserved, he kept modestly in the background. He was a more selective collector than his brother, concentrating on examples of the great printed books and volumes on the art of printing. The brothers worked together harmoniously. Their operations seldom overlapped except when a new book was to be created. Their books were never designed in the usual way — they evolved. An idea was suggested, a page was set, an illustration was made to be inspected and commented on by everyone in the shop. It would be revised or junked, and new proofs would be pulled. This would continue almost indefinitely until Bob would make the final decision and the trials would cease.

Ed Grabhorn's second marriage was to Marjorie Robertson, the daughter of John W. Robertson, a well-to-do San Francisco physician. While it solved Ed's financial worries, he could never quite forget the leaner years he had known. He was usually generous, especially with young aspiring printers, yet he was always worried about the wages he had to pay his employees. As a result he was happy to offer employment to numerous young people enamored by the prospect of working at the Grabhorn Press for meager wages or nothing.

William Bissell was one of those eager young volunteers. He was put to work at menial tasks, helping dampen the paper and distribute the type, when the brothers were printing their monumental *Leaves of Grass.* He and Bob became friendly, and it wasn't long before Bill introduced Bob to his sister Jane. Theirs was an immediate attraction. Bob was eleven years older than Jane, who was only about twenty at the time they first met. She was mature for her age and found this particular older man more interesting than any she had previously known. He enjoyed her wit and youth, and they were married on July 15, 1932. They spent their honeymoon in Europe and upon their return bought a comfortable cooperative apartment in Greenwich Terrace with Jane's dowry. They lived convivially there for the rest of their lives.

Jane's father was a formidable Army colonel. Her mother, Martha Bissell, was a true aristocrat in both demeanor and appearance. Life for the children in the Bissell household when Jane was growing up could be severe under the stern hand of their strict disciplinarian father. Andrew Hoyem recalls Jane's telling of an early childhood experience: "One day Jane, with her brother as an accomplice, coaxed their nurse into a wheelbarrow for a ride. The gullible woman was then set loose on an incline, crashing at the bottom to the delight of the children. Bruised and humiliated, the nurse limped to her employer with a report of the crime. Their father, an Army colonel who kept a large kennel, dealt with the culprits harshly. 'You have behaved like beasts,' he said, 'so I must punish you as I would my dogs.' Forthwith the children were chained to two empty doghouses. Her brother resigned himself inside his prison while Jane plotted revenge. Later that afternoon their father brought guests from the house to show off his pair of poorly trained animals. Jane bided her time and as the party approached the doghouses, she leaped out snarling and bit one of the guests on the ankle."

After Jane and Robert's honeymoon, Robert returned to the pleasurable drudgery of setting type at the press. Jane hovered about trying to keep occupied, sometimes proofreading, hounding delinquent customers, and handling much of the correspondence, which both Bob and Ed usually ignored. Her letters were often characterized by irreverent impudence as can be seen in this one to Jake Zeitlin: "My dear fellow: First, allow me to correct a fallacy of yours: solitary drinking is the only kind that is seemly and decent and dignified. One can't tattle, one can't gossip, one can't fight, one can't sentimentalize; one can't talk too much nor say too little, nor sulk, nor complain, nor make love to the wrong people.

"Ed will take fifty bucks for the Finn thing, if you will send it right away. Right away is a colloquialism and it means today.

"I enclose an order received from your Powell. You can't have the five Mark Twain books because they have not yet been issued nor will they be for some three or four months. I am desperately sorry, but there you are."

These simple chores failed to occupy all of her time, and finally, to amuse herself and to escape boredom, she began to putter around with the various types which were in such abundance on all sides of her. She had watched the brothers nif and naf as they would try to settle on the design for a book, and she decided that she, too, would like to experience the euphoria of creation. She set about it neither knowing nor caring about the traditional rules of typography. Once Robert had refused to let her buy a toy Jumbo press she'd seen in a shop window, logically explaining that they had a shop full of presses if she wanted to use one. When she finished printing her first piece on the shop's Washington handpress, she perversely dubbed her new undertaking "The Jumbo Press."

She set type with abandon, explaining, "It is the purpose of this Press to demonstrate that a layman may without help at all make a book." She broke words without regard, in the beginning or middle, running over even a single letter. She mixed types to suit her whim, composing her text as she set type. Not always being able to find the accessories she wanted, she wrote in jest that she was often obliged to "use pieces of old shoes, bits of fingernails, and chips off the radiators."

At another time, to further explain her concepts, she wrote, "Mad-abandoned — the Jumbo Press is revolutionizing the printing world, turning it upside down and topsy-turvy, exposing all its hoodoo-voodoo, and divesting its weird ceremonies of all their glamour. Jumbo stripped the mask from typography's Medicine Men and their disciples have seen them as they are: pompous, tottering pretenders, mouthing conceits and sweating decadence."

Jumbo became Jane's escape, her vehicle for self-expression during the rest of her life, as she sought personal recognition rather than being a shadow of the brothers Grabhorn. While she was quite aware of the prestige that accompanied the Grabhorn name, she continuously sought to escape and to create her own image. She once wrote, "Now Fine Printing is supposed to be so difficult that only Gutenberg and the Grabhorns ever really did it. But Jumbo has long scoffed at this myth. Jumbo Press says Printing is as easy as the Printer wants it to be."

Her new hobby was a joy and became her whole life. She explained, "Periodically, I think I would like to stay home, to keep house, to raise a family. I wonder whether I am not missing something. But I know I never will. I am so used to seeing my hands look like hell, to having a smudged face, and no time to get my hair fixed, to wearing dirty, frayed smocks. I am so used to printers and their jargon and their ways that I no longer care about anything else nor any other sort of people."

The Jumbo Press creations of Jane Bissell Grabhorn are not only delightfully original creations, they have become exceedingly rare collector's items. Some were done only as single copies and most were printed for a few guests on special occasions. She loved to create impudent keepsakes for these gatherings, especially for Robert's birthdays. For his fiftieth in 1950, she printed an amusing broadside nominating Robert as "Man of the Half-Century." Her text ran, "Married in 1932 to a pepper-and-salt-haired dipsomaniac of German descent whom he thought had money and a pristine copy of *The Tropic of Cancer*. Upon discovering the creature was destitute, and possessed nothing better than a dog-eared collection of Tiffany Thayer, he put her to work as 'prolonger' in the Grabhorn Press bindery, where she has remained ever since. She is never seen in public, and those few who have seen her report that she's prematurely crippled by hard work, with deep lines of suffering etched on her face. Grabhorn is said to have a mulatto mistress somewhere on Bush Street, but this bibliographer has been unable to confirm the rumor."

Years later, when Bob was 68, she printed an illustration of a young Bacchus and wrote, "Remember when you looked like this? Gee you were pretty and how I loved you dear old doll . . . loved your sinister cynical clinical evilly medieval ways. Now I know you had been to Paris, France, but then I was awestruck, me fresh from the convent and I thought I guess this is what they meant by Indianapolis Speed Ways."

As had happened so often before, Ed Grabhorn took on another young fellow as an apprentice for the summer to help out and enjoy the ambience and excitement of the busy shop. He was a student from Yale and a member of the Matson steamship family. His name was William Matson Roth. He was soon enchanted by Jane's wit, talent, and especially her Jumbo Press creativity. Sometime during the summer he suggested that he would agree to finance a new venture in publishing if Jane would participate. She accepted and the Colt Press was foaled in 1938 with Jane, Bill, and a friend, Jane Swinnerton, as partners in the new venture. Bill still had another year of college but was able to handle the editorial chores from New Haven. Jane Swinnerton was primarily a handywoman, leaving production and promotion in Jane Grabhorn's willing hands.

This new undertaking was completed separate from the Grabhorn Press, since the partners wished to establish their own identity. Jane wrote in an early prospectus, "The Colt Press passed from the conversational stage when its proprietors moved desk and typewriter into an office barely large enough to receive them. Small as it was, however, our office at 617 Montgomery was to us a triumph. We had an idea. The idea was we wanted to issue books that were beautiful, yet inexpensive."

These quarters soon proved too small, and they moved to Commercial Street. Jane wrote of the new quarters, "And here we sit, poor shivering colts, stoking our old woodstove, blowing on our cold little blue hooves to keep warm; and wondering how we can give you a beautiful book for $3.00."

Jane Swinnerton retired after a short time, and by 1940 the Colt Press books were being published by William Roth and Jane Grabhorn as sole proprietors. Roth had graduated from college and was giving his full attention to the press. They found their quarters on Commercial Street so uncomfortable that they moved their office back to Montgomery Street, which Roth observed "had the additional advantage of an unobstructed view of the Morgue."

Most of the books the press issued were printed by Lawton Kennedy, though some of the later ones were done in the East where the costs were lower. While Jane is usually given credit for the design of the Colt Press books, she relied greatly upon her husband's sure taste and Albert Sperisen's knowledge and artistry. Sperisen, a longtime friend, was the production manager of the Lord and Thomas advertising agency. Bill Roth remembers, "Things really began to hum as the team of Grabhorn, Grabhorn, Roth, and Sperisen would meet each afternoon at five to consider the day's problems, wrap up the last books for mailing at the Chinatown post office, and argue about the next book over Jacopett's twenty-five cent old-fashioneds."

The war brought an end to this fruitful collaboration. Sperisen went into the Air Force and Roth entered the Office of War Information, turning over to Jane his interest in and all of the assets of the Colt Press. Jane returned to the Grabhorn Press, once again to be isolated upstairs in the lonely bindery, away from the activity of the press. But she occasionally issued books with the Colt Press imprint, though they were now printed by the Grabhorn Press. Ed was innately averse to parting with cash, and he arranged with Jane to print Colt Press books in lieu of paying her bindery wages.

Among the many attractive books published by the Colt Press was a series of small cookbooks. For one of these, *The Epicure in China*, Jane had brazenly lifted the recipes from the food page of the *San Francisco Examiner*. Soon after the book's publication, the *Examiner* called to ask if it might be allowed to reprint her fine recipes in the food section, for which it was willing to pay her. She was happy to accept the offer.

In the early 1930s, when the Great Depression had effectively dried up the market for expensive press books, Ed Grabhorn began issuing a series of western Americana, stemming from his own interest and from his large collection of western material. The series was immediately successful and kept the press busy during those uncomfortable times. Jane, possibly at Robert's wise suggestion, undertook a similar series in the mid-forties called "The California Classics Series." Five titles were printed at the Grabhorn Press over a period of two years. The books were small in format, with attractive bindings of colorful printed paper sides and cloth backs. They were issued as limited editions of 500 copies and were out-of-print almost upon publication. A mere half-dozen more books were issued with the Colt imprint, the last in 1954.

The glamour and excitement of the early Grabhorn Press days had begun to fade by the late 1950s. Ed was in his seventies and tired. Sherwood Grover, who for some twenty years had relieved Ed of the tedium of running the presses, decided to leave for a better paying though less enjoyable job. This discouraged Ed, and surprisingly he turned down the offer to print three successive books for the Book Club. Bob was the only imperturbable one of the three. Jane was miserable. For the past decade she had been trapped in the bindery with seldom even a visitor. She felt unappreciated and was kept too busy to have time for any projects of her own. Jumbo was in abeyance.

In 1963 Marjorie, Ed's wife of thirty-six years, died. After a few months Ed disappeared. The next news of him that Jane and Bob had was a telephone call from Las Vegas telling them that he had remarried. Ed was then seventy-five. Jane was not very sympathetic toward this new relationship, and her comments were often caustic. Ed was annoyed, and there was a definite cooling in the relationship between the brothers who had worked together so harmoniously for over a half century.

The plant was closed as usual for the Christmas holidays in 1965. When Bob and Jane returned to work on the twenty-seventh of December, the place was padlocked with no explanation. Ed had decided to abandon the Grabhorn Press, and Bob and Jane were abruptly unemployed. It had been assumed by many that the brothers had been equal partners, but now it was revealed that Ed was the sole owner, and Bob, as he woefully admitted, was only a "favored employee."

The abrupt demise of this great press and the resulting alienation of the brothers was sad. Following the breakup, Bob found it necessary to sell his fine collection of books on printing to the San Francisco Public Library. He then formed a fortunate partnership with the young poet-printer Andrew Hoyem. The Grabhorn-Hoyem Press continued for seven years until Robert's death in 1973. Hoyem had managed to salvage most of the Grabhorn type for the new enterprise.

The Colt Press died with the end of the Grabhorn, but not Jumbo. Jane accompanied Bob to work each day at the new press. She helped with the binding for awhile but eventually was left to fritter the hours away on her own projects until it was time to leave for the day. Robert was always amused and quite proud of his wife's madcap creations, which he gathered for publication in a book, *The Compleat Jane Grabhorn, A Hodgepodge of Typographical Ephemera.* Included was the poignant "Jumbo's Lament."

I have tried in all ways
To be a perfect printer
I have never been swayed
By thoughts of fame or dinner
I have used white paper
I have used black ink
I have never catered
To what other people think.

But oh my Subiaco
Oh my Leaves of Grass
Oh my Kelmscott Chaucer
Oh my Golden Ass
I have never printed
A book that's worth a damn
I'm the kind of printer
That's jelly — never jam.

Jane was intolerant of stupidity. She was generous with her friends but contemptuous of most people. Her brother once asked Bob, "Why do you put up with Jane's outrageous behavior?" Bob answered, "Life would be so dull with anyone else." She had physical problems most of her life. She matriculated at Scripps College, but she had to leave in her second semester with an unfortunate illness. Later on it was discovered that she had nephritis or Bright's disease, and she was taken to the hospital to have a kidney removed. She wrote me, "I have been very sick since I last saw you. I developed Bright's disease, and as they were getting ready to operate, the X-rays showed that I was born with only one kidney. So it stays, of course, and the poor thing is not happy. It has been sadly abused."

Alcoholism blighted Jane's later years, but didn't dull her sense of humor. A couple of years before her death in 1973, she fell and broke her leg and was confined to her bed for some time. She spoofed the whole painful experience, writing, "How I broke my leg is I fell off a bar stool, which is all right. I have done it many times and none the worse for wear, as the saying goes. But I fell from the bar stool into a trap door, which had been carelessly left open by some workman, and into an open 100 gallon keg of beer. There I lay, thrashing about and hollering till I lost my voice. After about an hour of this I heard a voice from the bar upstairs (I cannot swear it was Bob's) shout, 'For Chrissake somebody shut that damn trap door, the noise is awful, can't hear myself drink.' The trap door was slammed shut and for several hours (I lost track of time) I languished in the beer keg, until mercifully I lost consciousness. But I had sustained this fearful compound fracture in my heroic efforts to extricate myself from the horrid dilemma in which I found myself."

Robert died not too long after Jane's recovery from this accident, and she followed soon after, but memories of a vibrant and always exciting friendship linger on. While I have dwelt upon the amusing and eccentric character of Jane Grabhorn, I have always had great admiration for her accomplishments and her graciousness to me. I certainly cherish her generous tribute, "Ward Ritchie's books are out of this world. Never a trace of ostentation, yet all the personality in the world. He is indeed a master." My own tribute to her is that she is unique among printers of all time. She has encompassed wit with beauty in a manner "out of this world."

# 7

## PARIS ADVENTURE
### WITH FRANÇOIS-LOUIS SCHMIED

---

*Schmied was the preeminent creative book printer and artist in Paris during the 1920s and 1930s. Ritchie was apprenticed to him during 1930 and 1931 and is able to give an intimate and firsthand account of the daily life in the atelier and of Schmied's method of work.*

---

AS A BOY, I was probably fortunate in growing up in a small town. The environment bred confidence and assurance that the future was mine, though that self-assurance was naturally tempered in later years by the realization that this journey in the best of all possible worlds was not always to be charmed. A half century ago, however, it would have been difficult to have convinced me otherwise. There was great beauty in southern California when I was a boy there. The air was fresh and clean, tinged only with the sweet smell of the orange blossoms and good things growing out of the rich earth. The mountains rose high to the north, with snow sometimes reaching down to the poppy fields that covered the foothills with their brilliant color in the springtime.

I was also fortunate in the children with whom I associated. When I recollect the successful careers of many of those with whom I spent my days in grammar school, I conclude that they too must have shared the youthful self-confidence fostered by our environment. Several of my boyhood friends, like myself, were influenced to devote their lives to books. This may have resulted from our early competition to be the first to read all the books on the shelves of the local library. Bill (William A.) Jackson became a respected bibliographer and director of the Houghton Library at Harvard University. Larry (Lawrence Clark) Powell became the University of California at Los Angeles librarian, dean of the School of Library Science, and author of numerous books about the lore of books and reading. Leon Dostert, a university professor and author, created the means of simultaneous language translation used during the Nuremberg Trials and later by the United Nations. I became a printer and publisher.

After graduating from college and spending a semester in law school, I became intrigued with the printing of beautiful books, and I quit law school to pursue this new goal. The Great Depression had already begun its long tenure, but I didn't realize its enormity. With naive self-assurance, I decided that I would work with the man I understood to be the most imaginative and creative printer in the world, François-Louis Schmied of Paris.

I first came across his name in volume three of *The Fleuron*, a journal devoted to the typographic arts. In an article entitled "The Book of the Future," J.P. Angoulvent wrote, "A few attempts have been made . . . none more instructive than those of the Parisian artist F.-L. Schmied. Two of his latest books, *Les Climats*, by Countess de Noailles, and *Daphné*, by Alfred de Vigny, may be considered as the most exact anticipations that can be given up till now of the book of the future." Also, in *A Catalogue of an Exhibition of Recent European Fine Book and Commercial Printing*, held at the Library of American Typefounders in 1926, Henry L. Bullen wrote, "Here we have the work of F.-L. Schmied, whom we regard as the greatest living master of the arts of the book. He designs and paints the illustrations, decorations, and initials of his books, reproduces his designs himself by the means of wood engravings, composes the types and mixes the inks."

After reading these heady encomia, I was eager to see examples of Schmied's books. This proved to be difficult. His books were printed in very limited editions, sometimes as few as twenty-five copies and seldom more than a hundred. Also, most had been printed only for members of one or another of the many exclusive book clubs of France, and few copies ever reached the United States. I was lucky. A petite, vibrant woman by the name of Alice Millard lived in a Frank Lloyd Wright house in Pasadena. The place was a museum of beautiful and expensive books. Her husband, George Madison Millard, had for years attracted the cream of Chicago area writers and collectors to his "Saints and Sinners Corner" in McClurg's bookshop. After his death, Mrs. Millard maintained his book business in California. She made yearly trips to Europe, returning with treasures to tempt wealthy California collectors. In Paris she had found a copy of Schmied's *Le Cantique des Cantiques,* which she later sold to Mrs. Edward L. Doheny, but not before she had let me study and enjoy it.

Schmied adorned his mature work in color and decoration, and this book is perhaps the best example of his uninhibited period. It is gorgeous in abundance and exuberance, unlike any book an American or English designer would ever do. There are no static pages in it — each opening is new and different, making it more art than book.

After satiating myself with the beauty of this book, I began to make my plans to get to Paris and, if possible, work for the artist Schmied. And a year later I was aboard ship for Europe. By a strange coincidence, I found on board a copy of a periodical called *l'Atlantique,* devoted to "Modern French Art Books and

Engravings." Looking through it I found an article about François-Louis Schmied, Painter-Engraver-Printer. It was a curious piece written in colloquial English, evidently with the help of a French-English dictionary. The description of Schmied is somewhat ridiculous, yet I can't resist quoting it: "The man is cut tall and wide, his regard is direct and placid. Noble, his aspect is evocative of figures and equilibrium. The virtue of his spirit is formed of enthusiasm, of impulse, of fantasy, of the imperious need of creative action, of curiosity, of divination. Who knows him loves him, and to know him is to dream of the legendary personages of far countries, noble, majestic and strong. His history is that of breaker of obstacles and of men with well-tempered hearts." It was written by a person who signed his name M. Taskin.

I arrived in Paris without a definite plan of action. With the confidence, or perhaps naivete, of youth, I hadn't thought it necessary. Fortunately I had a letter from Mrs. Millard to Mr. P. Byk of Seligman and Sons, from whom she had bought the copy of *Le Cantique des Cantiques*. He kindly forwarded a letter from me to Schmied, asking for a job. I received this in reply:

> Dear Mr. Ritchie: Mr. Schmied has just passed through Paris and has received your letter. Please excuse him if he do not answer himself your kind letter, but he was in great hurry.
>
> I can say on behalf of Mr. Schmied that his technique and conception of the art of book printing is for him absolutely personal, that it has needed thirty years of researches and training to acquire it and that consecutively if you want to be introduced to his *atelier* and share his processes, Mr. Schmied would ask you in exchange 6,000 fr. per month. I am, dear Mr. Ritchie
>
> Very truly yours,
> M. Taskin

I recognized the letter-writer as the person who had written the article in *l'Atlantique*. The letter erased my dreams of working with Schmied, but in the meantime, my old school friend Larry Powell arrived in Paris on his way to the University of Dijon to study for his doctorate. With Paris at our disposal for several weeks, I couldn't for the moment be too dejected. After September passed and Powell left for the university, I decided to go to England and see if Francis Meynell of the Nonesuch Press might be more amenable. All my arrangements were made to leave Paris, and my ticket bought, when, on my last day, I began to rationalize that this might be the only time I'd ever visit Paris and I hadn't even seen what Schmied's *atelier* was like.

I checked the address on the map, took the Metro to the Port d'Orleans, and walked until I finally found the studio of Schmied at 74 bis, rue Hallé. It was a narrow building several stories high and rather dingy looking from the street. There was a single door on the left on which I knocked and waited for a minute or so until a young chap opened it. My college French conveyed little more to him than I wished to see Mr. Schmied. I was ushered up the stairs to the reception room. On the wall was a bookcase filled with the books Schmied had designed and illustrated. There were several pieces of modern sculpture by the Hungarian artist Gustaf Miklos. As I was gazing around the room, a tall, broad-shouldered man appeared. Our attempts to communicate proved to be futile, and Schmied had to send out for an interpreter. M. Taskin was not on hand that day and I am certain that Schmied had no idea who I was or what I wanted, and that is why I was granted the interview. If Taskin had been around, I doubt I'd ever have seen Schmied.

The first question put to me by the interpreter was what I wanted. I explained that I had come all the way from California to work for Schmied. Schmied looked puzzled and asked where California was. That stopped me for a moment, and then I told him that it is where Hollywood is. This being clarified, a few more questions were asked, and Schmied shrugged his shoulders and walked out of the room, saying something to the interpreter. He turned to me and said that M. Schmied was perplexed, but since I had come all the way from Hollywood just to work for him, he could hardly send me back. I was to start work on Monday. And on Monday, no one was more surprised to see the young American than M. Taskin.

My first assignment was to hand-set some trial pages for a projected edition of *Faust* for which Schmied was preparing illustrations. I started out confidently enough, but I soon discovered something was wrong. Many of the letters that I was carefully picking out of their boxes in the typecase were not what I expected. It dawned upon me that the French typecase is arranged differently from the American. In addition to this disconcerting discovery, I also sliced off the tip of my finger on that first day. The French workers were most sympathetic and decided that they would have to protect me if I expected to survive. Schmied's older son, Théo, also took me under his protective wing. He was a couple of years older than I, a competent wood engraver and artist, enthusiastic, and on the verge of marriage, an event which took place only a few weeks after I began to work.

The wedding party was held at Schmied's home in the country, at Wissous about ten or fifteen miles from the city. All of the employees were bused there on the afternoon of the festivities. It was a beautiful day, with an abundance of champagne and food of all varieties arranged on tables around an enclosed patio. I enjoyed circulating and sampling many unfamiliar delicacies, while Schmied introduced me to the many generals, actors, and senators present. But in time I became quite uncomfortable as I couldn't converse with any of them. When M. Taskin, the only

English-speaking person present, planned to leave early to return to Paris, I decided to join him. Schmied refused to let me go. As a palliative I started sampling more of the champagne, which I had never before experienced, coming from Prohibition America. I enjoyed it. My communication improved, and I was soon dancing with all the girls and generally enjoying myself.

As I became more included in the activities of the family, in addition to my involvement in the *atelier*, I had the opportunity to learn much about Schmied and his work.

He was born in Geneva, Switzerland, on the eighth of November, 1873. His father had been a colonial in Algeria and was driven out by an Arab revolt. He, however, retained a nostalgia for the art and culture of this Mediterranean area, which he conveyed to his son. This, combined with a feeling for organization and geometrical precision from his Swiss-German forebears and his Gallic verve, explains in part the genesis of Schmied's art style. As a boy he studied at the Guillaume le Blé school, attracting the attention of Barthélémy Menn, who had worked with Ingres and was a friend of Corot, Rousseau, and Delacroix. He studied wood engraving under the direction of Alfred Martin, whose pupils also included Carlégle and Vibert.

After five years of copying the work of the wood engravers of the past, Schmied went to Paris in 1895 at the age of twenty-two. Photoengraving had not yet superseded wood engraving in book and magazine illustration. He made a living cutting blocks commercially, while engraving portraits and prints for his own pleasure. His ability as an engraver was recognized, and in 1910 *Le Société du Livre Contemporain*, one of the exclusive French book clubs, commissioned Schmied to engrave and print Paul Jouve's illustrations for Rudyard Kipling's *Le Livre de la Jungle.* World War I interrupted the project, and it wasn't completed until 1919. In the interim, Schmied had joined the Foreign Legion and was wounded at Capy on the Somme, losing an eye, which accounted for the dark glasses he always wore thereafter.

The production of *Le Livre de la Jungle* enhanced and altered Schmied's career. Jouve did finished drawings for only fifteen of the ninety illustrations, giving Schmied only a sketch and color indications for the remainder, which Schmied interpreted and executed, cutting almost a thousand blocks. Also the printer who had been commissioned to print the book wasn't able to print the illustrations satisfactorily, and through necessity Schmied acquired a press and became a printer. The reception and commendation Schmied received for his work on *Le Livre de la Jungle* resulted in several more commissions, which channeled his talents more and more into bookmaking.

With his purchase of a Stanhope handpress, Schmied also hired an incredibly competent pressman, Pierre Bouchet. On this rather primitive handpress were printed *Marrakech, Les Climats, Daphné, Le Cantique des Cantiques,* and *Deux Contes* before Schmied acquired more modern, machine-operated presses. These books are incredible examples of printing on a handpress. Sometimes twenty to twenty-five different colors, each printed separately from different engravings, were required to complete a single illustration. Anyone who has worked a handpress knows the difficulties of maintaining uniform inking and can appreciate the care necessary to produce these reproductions with the crisp, even type which accompanies them.

By 1925 Schmied's reputation as one of the outstanding and innovative French book artists led him to abandon his studio at 12, rue Friant and not only move to larger quarters on rue Hallé, but also to expand the operation. He was no longer involved in all the various aspects as he had been previously. He now had many working for him as engravers, composers, and printers.

The studio on rue Hallé, like most Parisian buildings in the older sections, was four or five stories high. The lower floor was devoted to the workshop. Facing the windows at the front of the room was a long bench at which four or five engravers sat cutting blocks. Théo Schmied, himself a fine engraver, supervised this operation and sat at the far right. Behind them was the Stanhope handpress and the cabinets of type. Between this room and the pressroom at the back of the building was a courtyard for occasional relaxation, where, in the fall, Schmied had us bottle his year's supply of wine from grapes he brought up from Monaco. In the pressroom there were three or four Italian Nebiolo presses, similar to our Colt's Armory or Laureate presses.

Up the stairs on the second floor was first the bindery, which had been installed not too long before my arrival. It was supervised by a man named Poéncin, aided by a couple of young Russian refugees, a brother and a sister. The bindings I saw were beautiful in their simplicity, often with no decoration on the rich black leather of the exterior but with a colorful lacquer of one of Schmied's drawings executed by his friend Jean Dunand as a doublure. Also on the second floor were the reception room and the library. On the third floor were dining quarters, the kitchen, and sleeping rooms. The fourth floor was for Schmied's studio and quarters, which no one ever saw. At least I didn't.

There was one rather incongruous and alien activity on the second floor — a small office from which a boxing promoter, a friend of Schmied's, operated. He managed quite a stable of boxers who would wander in and out. Many of them had fought in the United States, including "Kid Francis," who had quite a reputation in the States. It used to amuse Schmied when he would take a taxi home to find that almost every driver in Paris knew his studio as the home of the boxers and would treat him with great respect because he lived there.

Schmied loved people and embraced them in his great enthusiasm for life. He designed sets for the Théâtre Pigalle, tapestries for Gobelins, decorations for the liner *Normandie*. He was an officer of the Legion of Honor, and there were always a couple of generals and high government officials at his parties. He loved to introduce me as "the worst apprentice I've ever had" and then laugh and add, "and also the best and only one." One of his closest friends and patrons was Louis Barthou, member of *l'Académie Français* and one-time premier of France, who was later assassinated along with King Ferdinand of Bulgaria. But the most interesting of all was Dr. J.-C. Mardrus, the great scholar who translated *The Arabian Nights*. He and Schmied collaborated on many books. They are possibly the most perfect blend imaginable of the work of an author and an artist-designer.

Schmied was young at heart and especially enjoyed the company of Théo's young friends. At the studio in Paris he'd often have parties for these young people with music provided by an accordion player. Schmied was always the most active dancer and the youngest in spirit. The best parties, however, were at his place at Wissous. Here he entertained his friends from the world of art and politics. He would include his children and some of their friends, who were expected to furnish entertainment as the elders sat back and enjoyed their cognac and cigars. Dinner was always a prolonged affair. There were several hours of it, with course after course and wine after wine. The dining table must have been fifteen or twenty feet long. Over it hung a huge candelabra with at least thirty sputtering candles. It was hung by a heavy woven cord which could be lowered to replace the candles. Dinner always lasted longer than the candles, and midway a servant would come to affix and light a new set, which gave the guests the opportunity to relieve themselves and stretch their legs. After dinner the younger guests would gear up for the entertainment. There was a large closet full of costumes and props. We'd divide into two or three groups, each plotting a skit, and we'd vie for the most applause from the elders.

It was a year of unforgettable edification as well as pleasure for me. I had not worked in the *atelier* long before Schmied became concerned about my lean and hungry appearance and suggested that I join him and Théo for lunch every day. Soon he brought his daughter from Wissous to join us, and I was given the additional pleasant task of teaching her English. Lunch at the studio was almost as leisurely an affair as dinner at Wissous. Always, it seemed, we started with a dandelion salad, and each day Schmied would gleefully try to shock me by announcing that we were now enjoying *pissenlit,* which I translated into "wetting the bed." Usually there was a chicken or goose or other fowl, which I would watch Schmied strip with utter fascination. I doubt if any man ever did it as effectively and quickly. He would take his knife and slit the top of the breast, then grab the flesh between his finger and the knife and rip off the whole side. A couple more deft movements and the carcass was clean. There was always a roast or a ham to follow and quantities of the heavy red wine that we had bottled in the courtyard. I was convinced that Schmied retreated to his studio for a snooze after these lunches. I would have liked to, since I could hardly keep my eyes open during the afternoon.

Théo Schmied became my mentor and my closest friend, including me in his intimate group of cronies. We would gather from time to time with plans to revolutionize the world of art, literature, and theater. We were working on a play to accomplish all of this. I well remember one night in the studio of Claude Laurens, whose father was the sculptor Henri Laurens, when we tried to complete it. A fire burned in the woodstove. There was food and wine on the low wooden table. Claude's petite and beautiful Algerian mistress waited on us. The theme of the epic was somewhat of a mystery to me with my limited comprehension of French, but it vaguely had to do with the vision of the mind and the soul, to be treated symbolically with sets, ballets, costumes, and the play of lights. As far as I know, its production was never realized.

Jacques Chesnais was one of our group who later distinguished himself. At the time, he was working on the illustrations of a book to be published by *Les Éditions du Bélier* across the street from Schmied's studio. This was a project sponsored by Schmied, conceived as a means of helping and encouraging young artists by giving them the opportunity to illustrate a book. Four such books were published while I was there, including one illustrated by Théo, before the project was abandoned due to the Depression. Jacques' book was never published, but he turned to carving marionettes and writing plays and became the leading puppeteer of Europe.

I was indeed fortunate in being able to observe Schmied's techniques and procedures during the years when he was busiest and when his work was widely acclaimed and appreciated. His books usually took from three to four years to complete from the time of their announcement to their delivery. Beginning in 1921, a couple years after the publication of *Le Livre de la Jungle*, which had brought acclaim to Jouve and Schmied, they, together with Jean Dunand and Jean Goulden, held an annual exposition of their current and projected works in one of the major galleries in Paris. Here Schmied showed sample pages of books he had in progress or planned, and orders were taken. The books were limited and expensive, from $100 to $1,000, and there were variables for which one could pay even more, such as extra suites of illustrations or an original drawing.

The illustrations Schmied painted and the designs of the

pages for his books were explicit and precise. Everything was to exact size. The drawings had to be converted into wood engravings. The first step was to have the art photographically reproduced upon the end grain surface of a piece of boxwood. With the image clearly depicted on the block, an engraver would carefully make a master block. This was proofed on the handpress. While the ink was still wet, the proof would be placed in exact position on a clean block of wood, which would be put in the press and the image would be transferred to the new block. This would be repeated until enough blocks were prepared for each color required. From these, with the original painting in front of him, an engraver would cut away all the wood except that required to print one single color. I recall one instance where forty-five blocks had to be cut for the forty-five different shades of color required to reproduce a single illustration.

The actual printing was done as carefully. The early books were printed on the handpress, but the same care, and almost the same technique, was used later when the printing was done on a mechanical press. For exact register, the handpress method of points or pins was used. Two sharpened points like thumbtacks were fixed in position where the fold of the page would be. For the first impression, the placement of the sheet was carefully calculated and punctured into position. For each additional color impression it was only necessary to place the sheet with the pinholes on the points to get perfect register. It was a slow process. The press had to be stopped after each impression and the sheet inspected before another was placed into position. In many instances it would take a month to print a single page.

The problem of printing the often delicate plates on a rough-textured handmade paper or mouldmade paper was ingeniously surmounted by Schmied. As did John Baskerville a couple of centuries earlier, he had his paper heat-rolled, giving him a fairly smooth surface on which to print. Later on, if desirable, it could be dampened to restore its more natural rough appearance.

One of the aspects I most admired in Schmied's early books was the soft, velvety intensity of his black ink. It had a character unlike any other black ever printed. I asked him many times how it was made, but he was always evasive, telling me it was his own secret formula and would remain so. I am just as happy now that he kept it from me, as this deep black has damaged irreparably many of the early books in which it was used. Evidently he used too much linseed oil in his ink, and it penetrated the paper, blemishing some of his finest books, like *Daphné* and *Le Cantique des Cantiques.*

Although the American stock market had crashed in 1929, the Depression hadn't affected Paris to any great extent. But when I returned home in the fall of 1931, it was quite noticeable. It must have affected France soon afterwards, and especially printers like Schmied, who relied upon wealthy book collectors for their patronage. The books of Schmied and other art printers had been expensive, but they were considered a better investment than money in the bank. It was traditionally the responsibility of the printer to preserve the market value of his books. This was no problem during the expansive twenties and even the early thirties, but times and economics changed all of this quite abruptly. Schmied attempted to maintain the market value for his books in vain. He lost almost everything he had, and the next few years changed his life around. First to go, of course, was his beautiful sailboat, *Peau Brune,* with its multi-colored sails and its memories of great days sailing the blue waters of the Mediterranean. (When the firm of Seligman had an exhibition of Schmied's books in New York in 1927, many sold for exorbitant prices, some for as much as $10,000. With this money he had bought the boat.)

By the mid-1930s the studio on rue Hallé was closed, and things became quite desperate. Schmied's dear friend Louis Barthou and other friends in the government arranged to get him a post in the French territory of Morocco. Back in 1924 he had engraved the illustrations and printed on his handpress a book entitled *Marrakech,* about that colorful Moroccan city. His new assignment took him there, and beyond, to an outpost in the desert called Tahanaout. Here he created a miniature palace for himself from a deserted fort, painting its walls with colorful murals, planting flowers and trees, while bringing order and beauty to the place.

During the years of his exile he continued to create and paint. He illustrated a couple of books, which Théo printed, and made numerous paintings of the towns and dramatic countryside of this area of Morocco. Lucie Weill-Quillardet, the well-known French bookbinder, told me that she had gone to see Schmied in his isolated outpost almost 100 miles from the nearest railroad. She was probably the last and possibly the only European to have visited him. He kissed her with his former fervor, but she noticed that his hands trembled and he didn't seem to be too well. There was pestilence in the area, and as the "doctor and chief" responsible for his people, he hardly slept, being busy inoculating and taking care of them. She stayed only a few hours, feeling that she was intruding on his serious duties. Soon thereafter he died from the plague and was buried in the desert sand in a small mausoleum he had designed for himself.

# 8

## JOHN CAGE
### THE MANIAC OF MUSIC

---

*John Cage has revolutionized the concept of what is music by including
all sound, however dissonant and unpredictable. Ritchie met him in
Paris, and their paths crossed again in Mallorca, and later in Los
Angeles, when the Ward Ritchie Press was getting under way.*

---

IT WAS QUITE BY CHANCE that some time ago I turned the televi-
sion on to the Arts and Entertainment channel to a program of
Merce Cunningham's dance "Points in Space." I noticed that
the background music for the production had been created
by John Cage. There were some flashes of Cage at work. While
the round and youthful face had become elongated and gaunt
since the days I had known him more than fifty years ago, he
was recognizable, and the sight of him recalled many early
memories.

I first became aware of John Cage in 1929, though I didn't
actually meet him until a year later. He was a precocious sophomore student at Pomona College, only seventeen or eighteen,
rooming with Gregg Anderson, a friend of mine who earlier as a
page at the Huntington Library had helped interest me in printing. At the time I had a studio which Larry Powell and I had
rented in the Abbey of San Encino with the privilege of using its
printing facilities. One weekend Gregg visited me and set in

type a small announcement which he printed to distribute at the college. It was set without capital letters, which was considered *très moderne* and radical at that time. It read: "two whippersnappers believe that everything that is good is green, but that desirable things are not good. for this reason they are throwing away their books and want you to pick some up. besides they have seven watercolors by laudermilk that remind one of lemon satin dreams. there are drawings by the wife of the laudermilk. there is an etching, and there are stray copies of *blast, new masses, transition, new adelphi, hound and horn, ed howe's monthly.* the place to find all this is 347 west sixth street, claremont. you may not discover it on your first attempt, but it's there, right behind number 341. this shop has practically no hours. you may have to break in, but that is agreeable to the proprietors."

According to the Pomona College personnel records, when John entered as a freshman he was interested in the ministry, and he listed his interests as swimming, tennis, and riding. In his sophomore year he had changed occupational preference to writing and listed his interests as sleeping, talking, and stealing. He also mentioned in recounting his summer experiences that "I merely proved that I possess neither character, willpower, nor backbone." He decided to spend his junior year studying in Europe, and it was in Paris that I first met him. I had been working as an apprentice in the *atelier* of the artist/printer François-Louis Schmied. I received a note reading, "Dear Harry (I was known as Harry before my hair began to recede): I have a letter from Gregg Anderson saying: Go and see Harry Ritchie. My address is 15 rue de l'Yvette (16) Metro Station Jasmin. Sincerely, John Cage."

John's plans for his year of study in Europe were quite disorganized. He had many varied interests. He studied piano for awhile, became interested in Gothic architecture, and spent about six weeks from dawn to dusk at the Mazarine Library immersing himself in fifteenth-century architecture. About this time Joseph Pijoan, an art professor at Pomona, arrived in Paris and was horrified at his wasting time on ancient architecture. Pijoan arranged for John to work and study with Goldfinger, a modern architect. This job lasted a month, with John concluding that he had other interests than a complete devotion to architecture. He decided to go to England, but he made the mistake, when applying for a visa, of stating that he was planning to look for a job there. As these were depression days, his visa was denied. He confided in me that he was now at loose ends and wondered what he should do. I suggested that if I had time on my hands and no other plans, I'd love to explore the islands of the Mediterranean with all of their history and varied cultures. He liked the idea and was soon off to Italy and the island of Capri.

Some months later I was on the Spanish island of Mallorca, trying to shake off the chilblains with which the dreary winter weather of Paris had afflicted me. The warm paradise of Mallorca lured me there, not only for its climate but because it was the most economical place in Europe to live at that time. Alphonso XIII had recently been deposed, and the peseta had become a bargain when exchanged for American dollars. One could live luxuriously there on nickels and dimes. Not long after my arrival I ran into John in a bookstore in Palma. He told me that he and a young Harvard graduate by the name of Don Sample, whom he had met in Capri, had rented a large house at Son Vick, Bonanova, which was on the outskirts of Palma. The rent was only about $25 a month, which included a cook and housekeeper named Montserrat. John suggested, if I were willing to share expenses, there was a spare bedroom I could have. John was warm and generous with his offer. I have always suspected that his roommate was not too happy when I arrived with my suitcase. In my naiveté I remained unsuspecting of their relationship.

But living with them was a pleasant experience. They were intelligent, and both were interested in art and literature, as I was. The house was large and roomy, but could be quite drafty and chilly at night. There was a small library in which we would gather each evening to enjoy some rather strange cocktails which we ineptly took turns in concocting. We kept warm around an open brazier which glowed with blazing charcoal and radiated enough heat to thwart the chill. While the smoke was sometimes discomforting, the protective shield provided by our cocktails made that small discomfort tolerable.

We argued and talked of many things as I find in notes I made at the time. "Last night we gathered around the fire. I read some of Robinson Jeffers' poems and we started discussing whether Jeffers had anything new to say; whether the present time was ripe for any artist; is Spengler's philosophy a relic of the past and out of tune with the present. We talked on until one o'clock. John and Don went for a walk in the moonlight, but I was sleepy and went to bed."

Another time I wrote, "Today was bath morning. It is quite a procedure. Montserrat had to start a great fire down below the wash room to heat the water and then haul it up the stairs to the bath in many pailsful. I had to wait until eleven after John and Don had taken theirs together. That is how they always did it, they told me. That evening John read from *Tristram Shandy* about noses and we were amused. John is so much of a child — everything is nice to him — the poetry and painting of Don, the music he is composing. He is full of exuberance and shows a naive delight in art. I truly hope that something true and great will result for him. Don does not appeal to me. He is an egotistical and exacting Harvard type. Yet he has written a couple of quite nice poems, very modern. These two are like children, excitedly planning their trips together — through Spain, Morocco, India, Japan, and Mexico."

Perhaps the most memorable experience during my stay in Mallorca was the visit to the Seizin Press about which I kept the following notes: "John had heard of a press in Deyá, an English press, and we decided to seek it out. Our cook's brother had a car and drove us there. We sketched a bit on the way and arrived in Deyá about 1:30 in the afternoon. We saw a man in a blue sweat suit walking. We stopped to question him. 'An English printing shop you're seeking?' he questioned. 'It must be Robert Graves'.' He was German, but spoke enough French for us to understand, and gave us some vague directions. An old man with a bad eye followed us down the street to a *fonta* where we had some lunch and a bottle of very bad Spanish red wine. He sat patiently on a boulder across the road watching us as we ate. It was a prolonged lunch, as our hostess prepared all of our dishes from scratch. There was a big French boat and a German one in the harbor, so we whiled away the time watching the tourists being wheeled by in big sightseeing buses. Montserrat's brother was an affable fellow. On the trip over he had stopped at every *vista* to show us the beauties of his island — '*el buena vista,*' he would point out. He ate with us, greedily finishing all the remnants of our ample lunch.

"As we started for Sr. Graves' place, I filled John in a bit about Robert Graves and Laura Riding who lived and collaborated with him, and warned John that we might not be too welcome. The old man followed us expecting a few pesetas. We stopped at a house we thought to be Graves'. It was not, and we were directed to another which still was not right. This continued, and at each stop our little retinue was augmented by the curious householders. We had quite a crowd when we finally found

Graves' house. It was up a bank. I climbed the stairs and knocked timidly at the door. There wasn't an answer and I had retreated down the stairs when around the side of the house came a furious woman shouting '¿Qui es?' There on the embankment was a woman in a short khaki skirt with wild hair blowing in the wind. I asked meekly in English, 'We are looking for the English private press which we had heard was here in Deyá.' 'Who told you about us? Where did you hear about it?' she shouted. Perhaps her curiosity was what kept us from being summarily dismissed. She dispatched the crowd, including the old man to whom she gave a drink of cointreau as his wife was her laundress and this was the only way she could get rid of him.

"Now she turned to us and led us around to the back of the house to her study. She had been busy writing when we had disturbed her. Everything was in immaculate order with numerous leaves of manuscript around. We sat down and she began to cross-examine us. Where and how we had learned of the Press were her first questions. John explained that he had heard of it in the Snack Bar in Palma. She was furious and told us that Liam O'Flaherty had heard about them at the same bar and had come charging by with a hussy in tow, wanting to see Robert. She disliked people coming to see the 'great Author' while ignoring her. She had given him her tongue, suggesting that he take off his overcoat so that she could see if there was a man inside, and then sent him down to sit in his car while she served tea to his girl, who seemed surprised to find that great authors lived like ordinary people. She also dislikes Irishmen, which was another strike against O'Flaherty. I told her that we had no idea that it was their press until we arrived in Deyá, thinking it even might be Irish since at the bar there was mention of O'Flaherty's interest in it. To which she replied that if it were she'd tear up every book from it. And with this new grievance against the blabbering Snack Bar, she was determined to send Robert down to reprimand them severely. She detested people who came just to see the 'great man' and said that she was writing a pamphlet on just such an abuse at this very moment.

"And then naively she asked, 'Do you know who I am?' 'Laura Riding' I replied. This pleased her and she became quite affable. Then she wanted to know if we'd read any of her books. Our answer was no, though I had read some of her poems printed in *Poetry* under the name of Laura Riding Gottschalk. She said, 'They aren't printed any more in the United States, of which I am rather proud.' She added that Jonathan Cape in London would publish anything she wrote but the books didn't make any money — lucky to break even. I mentioned something about knowing Nancy Cunard. She replied that they were no longer on good terms. Nancy had printed one of her books without showing her proof sheets. She added that Nancy was leading a difficult life and thought that all of us living in our life-style should stick together. But Robert and Laura didn't feel that way.

"After she had thoroughly cross-examined us, which she did quite nicely, though bluntly, with smiles and laughter, she said she'd show us the press and then we could go. She led us into the house proper and into the library. There was a small handpress standing in the middle of the room with a title page locked onto the bed of the press ready to print. I asked many questions and found that they had the type set for them by a printer in Palma but did the press work themselves. She didn't consider it to be fun, just hard work. She also showed us copies of the several books they had printed as the Seizin Press and also the books Nancy Cunard had printed of their poetry. We were both so meek and modest and John so naive in some of his questions that she began to enjoy us. When she asked if we'd read any of her poems, John shyly asked, 'Would you like us to?' She thought this was a difficult question to answer and after a pause, didn't.

"I kept feeling that we'd intruded on her time too long and would say to her, 'I guess we'd better go.' She would agree but always seemed to find something new to show us. Finally we did start out through the kitchen when she stopped us to ask if we might like some tea. Our chauffeur had been patiently waiting all of this time. She suggested we send him to town for a drink while we enjoyed our cup of tea. The water in the teapot was cold so she wrestled with the kerosene stove, trying to get it to operate without any success. She finally offered us a glass of sherry to our delight, and was probably sorry she'd sent the chauffeur away.

"At about this time a large, loose-jointed man came lumbering up the steps and peered through the door at us. Laura brought him in and introduced us to Robert Graves. He was relaxed and amiable with a big boyish smile. He wore an old pair of white striped trousers, shoes that were patched on the top, and a supremely happy and contented look. He had been sunning on the beach. It took him no time to get the stove going and the tea ready. But Laura drank neither the tea nor the sherry, only water. She reviewed for him most of our conversation and then they got out some samples of the paper they were using. They questioned whether their Spanish paper could be handmade. Their English paper was made by Batchelor. They bought seconds for half price.

"They were extremely nice to us. Laura is a psychological study. She knows her own intellectual superiority and yet is overshadowed by Graves' prominence and resents it. She is American, 'technically American' she clarified. She'd been associated with the John Crowe Ransom group before she came to Europe. She doesn't like Paris. In fact she doesn't like any city, except possibly London. She is a vital person, and though she is not pretty and has stocky legs, I could envy Graves' relationship. Finally our chauffeur returned. They had me take him a glass of sherry and followed us down to the street to bid us farewell. Their final admonition was that if we mentioned to anyone we had come visiting, we should add that we had been thrown out. Laura remarked that the only reason she allowed us to visit was that we had asked to see the press, a concrete thing, rather than to get a sight of the 'great man.'"

I corresponded with both Laura and Robert after I returned to California, mostly with Laura. She had mentioned that she wished to write a poem in memory of Hart Crane and I told her I'd like to print it. She never managed to write it. Instead she sent me the manuscript of a poem entitled *Americans,* which I printed and had published by the Primavera Press. I wasn't aware of the consequence of our short visit upon Deyán affairs until several years later when Laura sent me a copy of *Focus. Focus* was an informal newsletter that she and Robert printed and circulated among friends, in which everyone commented about their current activities. Laura wrote as part of her contribution, "The only thing that has happened from America had been the publication of my ill-tempered, deliberately shabby little poem *Americans,* which I wrote a year ago for a rather nice young man called Ward Ritchie who has a press in California. He printed it beautifully with forthright red adornments, and now I am feeling somewhat shamefaced — on his account, not the poem's — because, without any suggestion of a whine, he has written to say how much he liked the *Leaves,* which I sent him, and how much he would have enjoyed being their printer. It was through Ward Ritchie, by the way, that the whole German situation arose here. He came to the village about four years ago, looking for the Seizin Press, mentioning my name and Robert's, and met the German called Herpes, who said, 'Oh, you mean Graves' press.'

When he found us he was surprised to see me, having got the impression that I was no longer concerned. Which of course started a thing with Herpes, who said, 'If a woman expects personal recognition, she shouldn't live with a man in the same house.' This went on to other bitter remarks, until one angry night Robert strode to the village and into the Café and slapped old Herpes' face. Whereupon all the Germans in Deyá were infected with a strong injured German-colony disease which has been passed on from one season's German colony to the next in true postwar spirit."

After returning from the continent in the fall of 1931, I worked for awhile in the bookshop of Jake Zeitlin. But when I was given the opportunity of printing a piece by Robinson Jeffers for *The Colophon* early in 1932, I started the Ward Ritchie Press with a minimum of equipment in a barn in back of my home in South Pasadena. When my mother died soon afterwards, the home was sold and I moved my type and press to an old farmhouse on Griffith Park Boulevard in Los Angeles. It became both living quarters and printing shop scrambled together. The walls were whitewashed pine boards, and there was a massive brick fireplace. An elaborate old chandelier with large candles hung from the ceiling to romantically help light the studio. A grand piano and an old grandfather's clock were mingled in with the type cases and printing presses. It was located only a few blocks from where the Disney Studios were then located and in an area swarming with young artists. The shop became the social center for the Disney artists and the others who'd drop by after work or during the day. It was appropriately dubbed "Ritchie's Roadhouse" by a frequent visitor, Lawrence Clark Powell.

I hadn't seen John Cage or Don Sample, except for one fleet moment in Paris, since Mallorca, and I was surprised to find they had rented a tiny house a block from my shop at the corner of Griffith Park Boulevard and Fountain Avenue. John's father was an engineer and inventor who lived in Pacific Palisades on the edge of the ocean just north of Santa Monica. He was not too pleased when Don and John returned from their travels and moved in with the family. Hence they had sought other quarters. Don was sickly and ever-complaining, with John waiting on him patiently. John also was again pursuing music and almost daily would come to practice on my piano amidst the bustle of a busy shop. The raucous clanging blasts and din of the printing shop's operations, mingled with the dulcet notes from the piano as John played, created a new sound of music. I have since wondered if this experience might not have influenced his later compositions.

John's relationship with Don Sample ended, and they left the little house down the street. I saw Don only once again when years later he was working on a WPA historical project. John began studying music seriously, first with Richard Buhlig and then with Arnold Schoenberg. Later in New York he did further study with Adolph Weiss and Henry Cowell. While John was still in California, in the middle 1930s, I was surprised and pleased when he married a quite plain young Russian girl from Alaska, Xenia Andreyeona Kashevaroff. I printed some stationery for her as a wedding present. There were a few restless years for them as they wandered, settling briefly in Seattle and Chicago before arriving in New York. I understand that they landed there destitute, with hardly twenty-five cents between them. Fortunately they had previously met Max Ernst in Chicago and he had mentioned that if they were ever to come to New York, they were welcome to stay with him. This they did.

John's early days in New York were ones of struggle. He soon forsook the ways of his teachers and branched into musical conceptions planned to shock, confuse, or amuse his audience. His programs were so bizarre that he soon gained a good deal of critical recognition and friendship with other contriving innovators such as Andy Warhol, Bob Rauschenberg, Jasper Johns, and Merce Cunningham. He became in short time the guru of the concept that there is music in all levels and variety of noise and dissonance, however jarring the sounds might be. He even created music out of silence, as in his well-publicized performance of "four minutes, thirty-three seconds." The orchestra sat in complete silence for that length of time as the audience's coughing, shuffling, and whispering supplied what was considered to be the music for Cage's experimental composition. The music critic Richard Kostelanetz wrote of it, "Thus Cage endowed unintentional noise with the status of intentionally produced music and broke the last connection with traditional definitions of musical structure." This piece was rudimentary among Cage's creations. His more startling compositions consisted of more contrived and complex arrangements of noise. Early in his career, in 1945, during the war years, *The New Yorker* in "Town Talk" reported how "he organized a percussion orchestra composed of such inharmonious instruments as tom-toms, wooden blocks, bells, gongs, cymbals, anvils and automobile brake drums." Cage explained that he was holding back some of his most effective sounds from this performance until after the war, saying, "They are too frightening. They sound too much like the scream of bombs, and planes, and rifle shots. It wouldn't be good taste to use them now. One of them even shocks me sometimes."

In the following years Cage developed an even greater confusion of sounds as, for example, in his "Walk with the Dancer." *Time* describes the performance: "Composer Craig's electronic nightmare lasted ten minutes and required the services of Cage himself, Pianist David Tudor and Dancer Jill Johnson. Occasionally reading directions from slips of paper, they scurried from one short-wave radio to another, twiddling dials and assaulting the audience with a drumfire of rattles, bangs, pops and nonsense syllables roared into a microphone. Occasionally they turned on an electric blender or belabored the piano. Before 'Music Walk' began Cage had no idea how it would sound, had determined only that it would last ten minutes, involve certain props and three performers doing more or less as they pleased. It was a prime sample of what students of the avant-garde call 'indeterminate' music, *i.e.*, music that is based on almost pure chance."

Through such contrived creations, Cage has achieved the status of "The Grandfather of the Avant-garde." While he often, intentionally, plays the part of a buffoon, he is more profound than these antics would indicate. While I watched Cunningham's "Ballet in Space" and carefully listened to Cage's accompanying music, I was impressed by its subtle restraint. It consisted of heavy breathing, silence, a gasp, and an occasional gurgle, accompanying but never intruding into the dancing. Cunningham termed his creation not dancing, just moving around. Cage called his, not music, just sound.

John Cage's antics have served him well, and while most of his compositions are impermanent, meant to be one-of-kind improvisations, he has been acclaimed as the foremost exponent of nonmusic and possibly one of the most innovative creators of this time.

# 9

## ST. JOHN HORNBY
### AND THE ASHENDENE PRESS

*C.H. St. John Hornby's Ashendene Press was, along with William
Morris' Kelmscott Press and Cobden-Sanderson's Doves Press, one of
the great classic presses of the "Revival of Printing" in England.
His story of his press as recounted to the Double Crown
Club in England is included here.*

IT WAS THE SPRING of 1931 that I first saw Charles Harry St. John
Hornby. I'd been working as an apprentice in the *atelier* of
François-Louis Schmied in Paris, and before returning home to
California, I spent a few months in England. It was then that St.
John Hornby invited me to tea at his home, Shelley House on
Chelsea Embankment. I arrived at this impressive house near
the bank of the Thames and hesitantly knocked. While I was
waiting another young man arrived, also expected for tea. He
introduced himself as Philip Hofer from the New York Public
Library. The door opened and we were ushered up the stairs to
the library where Mr. and Mrs. Hornby greeted us with English
warmth.

While chatting and awaiting tea we had an opportunity to
look around, with Hornby showing us a sampling of his collection of early manuscripts, all in as near perfect condition as
could be found. He mentioned that he would never buy a book

or manuscript that wasn't immaculate. The room was lined with books, and on one of the walls above the bookcases hung the oar he had used as a member from New College of the winning Oxford crew in their race against Cambridge in 1890. It was proudly signed by all of the members of his crew. There were many small tables in the room on which were neatly displayed a selection of manuscripts and beautifully carved and inlaid boxes. One was inlaid with his many rowing medals.

After tea we descended into the garden in back of the house and to the small building he'd built for the press. There was a trickling stream running through the property, and Hornby pointed out where Nell Gwyn, the mistress of Charles II, was said to bathe in the nude. Inside we were introduced to the pressman who was printing the first pages of *Thucydides* on an Albion handpress. A compositor was setting trial pages of *Daphnis et Chloe*, which Hornby rather sadly told us would probably be his last book except for a bibliography. He said his pressman of many years was getting too old to enjoy the work anymore, as he also was, and he couldn't face the task of training a new one. I asked him if he ever operated the press and he answered, "No, I used to set the type but now I only check the proofs and frame the pages." Mrs. Hornby mentioned that he'd usually spend some time at the press early in the morning before leaving for work and occasionally after tea and on Sundays.

We returned to the library to be shown some of the rarer Ashendene books, including three copies of the early printed *Songs of Songs* on vellum. Each copy had been individually decorated by Florence Kingsford, who later became Mrs. Sydney Cockerell. The decorations of the forty copies printed had taken Miss Kingsford a year and a half to finish. Hornby had kept five copies, with these three still in his possession. Cockerell also had five copies. We were then shown copies of his first two books. They were not well-printed, but at the time he printed them, he was inordinately proud of his accomplishment and immediately sent a copy to William Morris. Morris thanked him and wrote him that it was nicely done. Hornby gratefully remembered this and later was similarly generous to the many young printers, including myself, who would send him examples of their work.

Hornby had been asked to address the Double Crown Club on the occasion of its thirtieth meeting. I had been invited as the guest of Francis Meynell, and being a stranger to English customs, I assumed it would be formal. I arrived at Kettner's Restaurant in black tie and tuxedo and was quite embarrassed to find everyone in informal dress. A little later Philip Hofer arrived, the only other American guest. He was also in his tuxedo, which led our English hosts to conclude that life in the colonies was much more formal than theirs.

In addition to this embarrassment, Francis Meynell had not yet arrived, and I stood at a loss in a crowd of strangers until St. John Hornby noticed me. He took me to meet Graily Hewitt. We chatted and looked at some of the Ashendene books on display for which he had done the initials. When I mentioned that I'd like to take some lessons in lettering from him, he told me to buy his book which would teach me as much as he could and would be far less expensive.

Dinner was announced and Meynell still hadn't arrived so Hewitt guided me to Holbrook Jackson, the social chairman, who found my place. I was immediately attracted by the menu which Bruce Rogers had concocted from printer's flowers. It showed squirrels abandoning a barren tree for those with an abundance of nuts.

I felt almost as abandoned as that poor tree, but Meynell, together with Bruce Rogers, finally arrived. They explained that they had been unavoidably detained at a cocktail party, which seemed to be a valid excuse.

It happened that we had an extremely congenial group at our end of one of the tables. Besides Rogers and Meynell, John Carter, who was Rogers' guest, sat next to me; Oliver Simon was across the narrow table with Philip Hofer. I was in awe of the many great printers there as I looked around the room. I had originally been seduced into a career as a printer by reading *The Journals of Thomas James Cobden-Sanderson.* His son Richard was there and invited me to dinner at his home in Hammersmith on the bank of the Thames where the Doves Press had been. Across the room was John Johnson. His appearance intrigued me. He was slightly paunchy with straight silken brown hair that hung over his forehead in bangs reminiscent of Aubrey Beardsley. I held him in great admiration. We corresponded regularly over the years. At one time he wrote me, "We still have books in type, or rather fragments of books in type, which have been slowly moving their appointed course for twenty or thirty years. And so conservative is this university, that I always call the file-copies of the previous day's printing, which flow before me at ten o'clock every morning, the pageant of printing of the last fifty years.

"But the good Bruce Rogers knows us inside and out and will tell you what manner of men we are. We are a rather stern factory of nearly 900 souls, and to very few is given the privilege of wandering in and out at their own free will. But Bruce Rogers has that privilege. And Bruce Rogers has never quite forgiven me for using the expression 'wayward' in that little Dent lecture which I gave. The truth is that he is and he isn't wayward.

"But I don't like his punning version of the *Bible* page, although I know very well it gave his queer punning instincts a great deal of satisfaction in the making of it."

I had wanted to meet Emery Walker, whom Meynell had

earlier assured me would be there. But he was ill. My disappoint-
ment led Rogers, whose office was in Walker's quarters in Cliff-
ord's Inn, to suggest that I drop in on him the next morning, as
Walker would in all likelihood come to work. I was there bright
and early, but Walker was still too ill. However, I had a delightful
three hours with Rogers while he was checking the proofs of his
*Bible.*

I was all ears and wide-eyed with the heady conversation at
our table, somewhat abetted by some of that great wine the
English seem to be able to extract from their French neighbors,
when Michael Sadleir introduced Mr. Hornby. I am sure that all
present knew the great books that had come from the Ashendene Press, but few could have anticipated the warm and
informative talk that followed. Hornby stood tall and handsome as he spoke, softly and modestly:

———————

When I undertook to read a paper upon my Private Press
before this august assembly of printers, I rather underestimated
the difficulties with which I should have to contend. It is not easy
to make such a paper interesting to a body of expert typographers who could probably teach me a great deal more than I
could teach them, and in any event it is always difficult to talk
about printing without the help of slides. But possibly some
short account of the books I have produced and the difficulties I
have encountered may be of some interest even to past masters
of the craft. By way of preface I should like to say that I did not
start on my career as a printer of books with any high-flown idea
of showing how it should be done. My beginning was essentially
a humble one. I had no thought of, or desire for, either fame or
profit. Such fame as may have come to me has been entirely
unlooked for and unsought, and no one was more surprised than
myself at the growing keenness of collectors to possess speci-

mens from my Press when they became obtainable. I say this, because it is sometimes objected against us so-called Private Press people that we set ourselves up as superior to the ordinary printer. This may be due to the fact that of recent years the Private Press has been over-exploited owing to the readiness of a certain type of book-buyer to absorb anything that has rarity value. It is a form of collecting which personally I strongly deprecate, and I never myself buy a book for this reason unless it has some other merit to commend it, or possibly unless, being itself below standard, it is part of a set which is as a whole desirable. And furthermore, though a handpress printer myself, I do not claim that the work of the handpress is essentially better than that of the machine or even that hand composition is better than the best work of, for example, the Monotype. The most that can be claimed by the Private Press owners is that they have tried to set and maintain a high standard of book production and to apply to it the right canons of taste and proportion together with a use of the best materials available. So far as the former is concerned I think that their influence has been good. The question of the use of good materials is to some extent, though by no means entirely, one of cost. Many books, as we know, are spoilt by the use of unduly thick paper when a lighter quality might have been used at no greater cost.

Such good influences as Private Presses may have exercised upon printing in general have been gained rather by suggestion than by direct imitation of their work and methods. It is impossible when speaking of Private Presses not to allude to the Kelmscott Press. Now, whatever our opinion may be about the beauty of the types designed by William Morris and the books produced by him, I think that we shall all certainly agree that there were present in his work all the essentials of good book-making — good paper, good ink, even presswork and above all nice proportion in the imposition of the printed page. We may disagree about his ideas of decoration. Personally I think that the Kelmscott *Chaucer* is in many ways the greatest example of a printed book of all time. But it is inimitable. Morris was a genius. We can admire him or not but we cannot copy him. Witness the lamentable attempts which have been made both here and in America to do so. But we can follow the spirit of his work, and that spirit has without a doubt exercised during the past forty years an enormous influence upon printing throughout the world. Even those who profess to make light of Morris as a printer are themselves largely influenced by what was best in the Morris tradition, just as he was himself influenced by the splendid manuscript books of the Middle Ages and by the masterpieces of the fifteenth-century presses.

A Private Press such as my own works under severe limitations. In the first place there is a limit of time one can give to it. In the second place there is the limit of material — in the way of type. It is impossible for these reasons to try many of the experiments in typography which have been so successfully tried by many larger and better equipped printing offices. Although, if I had had the time to give to it, I should have delighted in making such experiments. I was not really greatly concerned by these limitations, because my own taste in book production inclined towards following the tradition of the earlier printed books of about 1470, where the same limitations of material existed. And although for this reason the problems I have had to face have been comparatively simple, I think that most of you who are printers will agree with the words of the well-known American printer, Theodore Low De Vinne, when he says the important thing is to space words evenly, to put proper blanks between lines of display so that any reader can see at a glance that the whole book is the work of a disciplined hand and educated taste, and that proper subordination has been maintained in all the little details, from the space between the words to the margins around the page. These, I think, call for more of skill, more of experience than are required to create the most difficult pieces of ornamental typography. I have said nothing about the difficulty of keeping even color, exact register, and absolute cleanliness in presswork. I might go on and enlarge on this more. If any amateur or novice thinks that the printing of a good plain book is a simple matter, let him try. A year of experience will make him "a sadder and wiser man."

Perhaps the best case for the amateur printer is made by Stanley Morison, one of our greatest, if not our greatest, authorities on printing. In this assembly I make no excuse for quoting his words from *Four Centuries of Fine Printing,* as they express better than I myself could what I feel about so-called fine printing.

"The *fine* printer begins where the careful printer has left off. For *fine* printing something is required in addition to care — certain vital gifts of the mind and understanding. Only when these are added to a knowledge of the technical processes will there result a piece of design, *i.e.,* a work expressing logic, consistency, and personality. Fine printing may be described as the product of a lively and seasoned intelligence working with carefully chosen type, ink, and paper . . . First it must be borne in mind that a fine book is more than 'something to read.' The amateur looks for character in printing. The book therefore which essays to rank above the commonplace will, while not failing in its essential purpose, carry the personality of its maker no less surely than that of its author and its subject. The problem of the typographer is to achieve an individual book without doing violence to its essential purpose or to any accidental character conferred by an artist or book decorator. Thus the whole mystery of fine typography lies in the perfect reconciliation of these interests. Moreover, there is no master-formula; almost every other book is a challenge to the artist-typographer."

To return to my own Press. Why did I ever start as an amateur printer? It is difficult after thirty-six years to give a clear answer. I hardly know myself. I really started, I think, for the fun of it and for no other reason. I had always been fond of books, for their form as well as for their contents, and I had always been fond of working with my hands. I happened at the time — the autumn of 1894 — to be spending a few months in the printing works of W.H. Smith & Son in Fetter Lane, learning the business, and I thought I would like to set up type. This led me on to pulling proofs of what I had set up. I had a friend at Zaehnsdorf's the bookbinders, A.L. Marlow, who one day offered to take me with him on a visit he had arranged to the Kelmscott Press at Hammersmith, whose books I had just begun to admire though I could not yet afford to buy them. There I spent a never-to-be-forgotten afternoon seeing the sheets of the *Chaucer* being printed on the handpress, culminating in an hour's talk with the great Morris himself in his library, which was also his work-room. Then there was tea at the great oak table in the dining room presided over by his still wondrously beautiful wife. From that day forth nothing would content me but to have a Press of my own. I had no idea of rivalling Morris, but I wanted to print a book, be it ever so small. I knew that printing for me could never be the serious occupation of my life but merely a byplay for such leisure time as I wanted to devote to it. And since that day I can say that, with the exception of about three years during the war, I have devoted a great deal of my leisure time to my Press and have derived from it the greatest pleasure. My first step was to find a home for the Press. I happened at the time to be living at my father's place, Ashendene in Hertfordshire, and in the garden was a summerhouse with a little room about ten by five feet used for storing odds and ends. I cleared out this little den and annexed it. In it I fitted up a secondhand Albion Crown Press purchased from John Esson & Son in Fetter Lane and set up two case racks of type and a small imposing stone. My ink table was an old lithographic stone and my first font of type was about eighty pounds of Caslon old face pica. The whole outfit involved a capital outlay of some thirty-six pounds, which for me at that time was a considerable sum.

I chose for my first book a fragment of a diary kept by my grandfather during a short visit he made to Paris during the spring of 1815. (It is of interest to note that I am tonight wearing the watch he bought from Le Roy on that occasion, which after 116 years is still going strong.) The diary breaks off with the announcement of Napoleon's escape from Elba and the traveller's hurried return to England. This little book, of which a copy may be seen in the adjoining room, is from every point of view, except perhaps the margins, a sorry piece of work. The composition is poor and the presswork lamentable. It was printed on dry paper and the ink was inferior stuff. I had learned nothing about make-ready and the colour is faint and uneven. Nevertheless I was very proud of it at the time and thought it rather a fine effort. I had to feel my way by experiment and I was in no wise discouraged.

My second production was *La Vita Nuova* of Dante. For this I used a long primer type from the Oxford University Press, with some dreadful capitals culled from a type-founder's catalogue. The use of these was suggested by Morris himself, and he was kind enough to say that he thought it was nicely done. I have often thought of this when I have had to return thanks for similar gifts from budding Private Press owners. Morris himself, I regret to say, did not long survive the gift. For this book I used a Japanese paper on which it was easy to print, and the presswork shows a marked improvement. I did five large paper copies on a handmade paper. These, needless to say, showed every fault of marginal proportion and were a warning to me for the future. So-called large paper copies were in fashion at the time, but I never repeated the experiment. In the setting up of this book I had the assistance of one of my sisters, and she with two other sisters helped me in setting several of the subsequent books. The work was done a few lines at a time whenever I could snatch a spare half hour, and the presswork was generally done on Sunday mornings. It called for some enthusiasm, as I had to do everything myself, including the dirty work of washing up. For this book I used my first press mark, printed in red.

*La Vita Nuova* was followed by a little *opusculum* printed for the Sette of Odde Volumes, of which I was then a member. It was printed on a handmade paper, undamped, in Caslon pica with long primer shoulder notes. I tried dampening the paper, but was so troubled by the cockling of the sheets that I had to print "dry." I soon began to want a type rather more distinctive than those which could be bought from the typefounders. In those days there was nothing like the fine range of types to be had today. I got an introduction to Horace Hart, printer to the University of Oxford, and he kindly undertook to cast for me by hand two small fonts of Fell great primer and english. These types, after lying dormant for over a hundred years, had been resuscitated by Dr. Daniel of Worcester College for use by his Private Press. Though not particularly beautiful they have a certain rugged distinction and seemed to me more suitable for a Private Press than any of the types then in commercial use. I added two further Fell types later, one of small pica small caps and one black-letter. With these Fell types I printed ten books, including *Three Poems of John Milton, Three Elegies, Rubaiyat of Omar Khayam, The Book of Ecclesiastes,* and *Aucassin and Nicolette.* After my first three books I was not satisfied with the ordinary paper obtainable, so I went to Batchelor & Sons and got them to make me a paper on special moulds. This bears a watermark of a bugle-horn, my family crest, and I used this paper for all the books printed at the Press between 1896 and 1900.

I had a good deal of difficulty with the dampening at first as I found, as I had found before, that the paper cockled badly. Eventually I got over this by using interleaving sheets considerably larger than the paper itself. These I dampened with a sponge and left under 112 pounds pressure for twelve hours, afterwards interleaving the printing sheets and leaving them under pressure for a further twelve hours. This is the method I employ to this day. I also at this time in 1896 procured a really good ink from the firm of Janecke & Schneeman of Hanover. My presswork from 1896 onwards showed a marked improvement, but I always labored with the disadvantage of having to do my work at odd times, whenever I could snatch a spare hour or two. This naturally did not conduce to the best work and I am afraid that my books savoured of amateurishness in many ways. But I did not profess to be anything more than an amateur. I was printing entirely for my own amusement, and such little books as I did I gave away to my friends and others whom I found were interested in the Press. I did not offer any to the public. I received some encouragement from American collectors, but very little in this country.

At the end of the year 1900 I moved my Press from Ashendene to Shelley House in Chelsea where it has been ever since. Here in the corner of the stable yard at the back of the house I built a small workshop of three rooms. On the ground floor is the composing room and above are two small rooms, one of which contains the press while the other is used to store paper. The first book printed at Chelsea was Andrew Lang's translation of

*Aucassin and Nicolette* in Fell black-letter. This was followed by
*The Revelations of St. John the Divine,* also in black-letter. My first
experiment in printing on vellum was made with this book, but
whether it was my fault or the fault of the vellum, it was a signal
failure, and no perfect copy of the book appeared. I still have one
or two vellum sheets of this book to remind me of my want of
success.

A turning point in the history of my Press was my meeting, I
think in the year 1901, with Sydney Cockerell, who, as most of
you probably know, had been for some years secretary to the
Kelmscott Press. Through him I got to know Emery Walker,
whose name deserves to be held in honour in any gathering of
printers. These two men, who have for thirty years been among
my closest friends, gave me encouragement and unstinted help
and advice. Cockerell was an unsparing and outspoken critic.
Walker was a mine from which to draw a wealth of counsel, ever
at the free disposal of any struggling beginner. I owe both of
them a debt I can never repay. And I am only one of many whom
their kindly enthusiasm has fired and guided toward better
things. My long talks with them made me ambitious to have a
type of my own, which Walker's knowledge made possible.

I consulted with the omniscient Robert Proctor at the British Museum and, after examining numerous fifteenth-century
books, decided that I would like to have a type modelled upon
the Subiaco type of Sweynham and Pannartz, with which three
books had been printed in 1465 before these printers moved to
Rome. Morris at one time made experiments with this type but
never went so far as having it cut. Walker and Cockerell, who
were then in partnership, made photographs for me from a
vellum copy of Cicero's *De Oratore* in the British Museum. My
type was cut by E. P. Prince and cast on a great primer body by
Miller & Richard. In these days of high prices it may be of inter-

est to record that the total bill for photographing and cutting amounted to only 100 pounds. I was a very proud man when the first dozen letters reached me and I was able to set up a few specimen lines. I still think, as I thought then, that it is a very noble type. Its possession made me ambitious to produce something more important than I had hitherto done. I bought a larger press and had a new make of paper of larger size and decided to print *La Commedia di Dante* in three small octavo volumes. Of these the *Inferno* appeared in 1902. It was the last book done entirely by my own hand, and it gave me many a hard day's work. I had some help in the setting-up from a cousin of mine and neighbor at Chelsea, Meysey Turton, who used to come in the evenings after his work in the city.

The setting-up and printing of 150 copies of this book was a very heavy tax on the spare time of a busy man, and I decided that I must either give up the idea of producing important books or take on a regular pressman. I decided on the latter course and engaged George Faulkner, who had had his training at the Oxford University Press and who is with me to this day. He required a good deal of licking into shape but eventually developed into a very good and careful pressman. I did not engage a regular compositor, continuing to do most of the setting-up myself with the help of my cousin and Faulkner, whom I taught and who luckily, in those days, was not trammelled by a trade union. Since the year 1910 I have had a regular compositor, but I have continued to this day to do all corrections myself and make up all the forms for printing.

With the appearance of the *Inferno* of Dante I made another change in the policy of the Press. Hitherto, as I have said, I did not issue my books to the public. But I found that there was a growing interest in them amongst collectors, and I was continually getting letters from people anxious to acquire them. I could not give away copies to all and sundry, so I came to the conclusion that the only thing to do was to issue a prospectus in the ordinary way and accept subscriptions. There is really no other way of getting books into the hands of those interested in them. The expenses of the Press, with its more ambitious programme, were growing and might grow still further. I had to think about recovering at least some of them. I do not know how other Private Presses have fared, but I think it may interest you to know that after thirty-five years, throwing in my services for nothing, I am about "all square" without profit or loss. I hope, therefore, that I have given good value for the money. The profit I have had, and it is a rich return, is the immense interest and pleasure I have gotten out of the Press. For the consolation of others who may be thinking of following in my footsteps I might add that I have probably run my Press rather extravagantly and that there may be something to be made out of a Private Press in these days by anyone who does really good work and who is indifferent to whether or not any profit will result. But I should not advise the venture as a quick road to fortune even though it may lead to fame.

After the *Inferno* came *The Song of Songs,* of which I printed forty copies all on vellum. Every one of the copies was illuminated by Florence Kingsford, now Mrs. Sydney Cockerell, and many of them are very beautiful.

The year 1903 saw the issue of three books — two little volumes of the Alcaic and Sapphic odes of Horace and Dame Juliana Berners' *Fysshyngwyth an Angle.* The same number appeared in 1904, including the second volume of the *Commedia.* In this year for the first time I included original woodcuts in one of my books — a collection of stories from the *Fioretti* of Saint Francis. These woodcuts were done after drawings by Charles Gere and engraved by W.H. Hooper, who had done the cuts for the Kelmscott *Chaucer* and whose hand had not lost its cunning though he was far advanced in years. He had, I believe, been one of the early wood engravers on the staff of *Punch*. He continued to work for me until his death, which took place when I was halfway through my *Morte d'Arthur,* about the year 1911.

I had already used woodcuts, though not original ones, in my edition of the *Commedia*. These were taken from the Venice edition of Dante's *Commedia* of 1497, which in their turn had been copied from the 1481 edition. I had these redrawn and modified to suit my page by Mr. Catterson-Smith, and they were cut for me by Charles Keates.

The initials at the beginning of each canto of the *Commedia* and each ode of the two Horaces were done by hand by Graily Hewitt in red, blue, and green. Since 1902 Graily Hewitt has been a constant collaborator in my books. In addition to doing by hand the initials for the *Commedia,* the Virgil, the Horaces, and the *Lucretius,* he has designed for me several alphabets of initials and numerous initial words, the latter used chiefly in two volumes of Spenser and my latest book, *Thucydides.*

In the year of 1904 Eric Gill designed for me an alphabet of capitals, and these I used in the *Fioretti* of that year and in More's *Utopia* in 1906. In this latter year I started upon what was for me an "opus magnum" and was in fact a considerable work for a single handpress and one pressman. It was *Tutte le Opere di Dante.* I believe that no edition of all the works of Dante existed in one volume except that printed in very small type by the Oxford University Press, the text of which was prepared by Dr. Edward Moore. I got permission to use this text in my edition. I decided upon a folio size with the pages printed in double column as best befitting the majesty of Dante. The volume contains six woodcuts by Hooper, after drawings by Gere. The large initials printed in red are all from designs of Graily Hewitt. This book took me three years to print. It was issued in 1909 and brought me a certain amount of fame. Looking back at it now, after twenty years, I still feel that it is a good bit of work and not unworthy of the "altissimo poeta."

Having printed the Dante I turned to his great master, Virgil, and printed an edition of forty copies on Japanese paper and six copies on vellum. The number printed was of necessity small because all the large initials were done by hand by Graily Hewitt along with hundreds of paragraph marks in red and blue in each copy. Meanwhile I turned my thoughts to another folio and selected Malory's *Morte d' Arthur,* which occupied me for the following three years. For this book I had some thirty drawings done by Charles and Margaret Gere and cut on wood by W.H. Hooper and J.B. Swain. Graily Hewitt designed for me a new set of large initial letters, and for the first time I used blue, alternately with red, for the printing of the initials. Taken as a whole I think this is one of the best of my books, though some may think that the line is rather long for the size of the type. I have a particular affection for the volume that followed it, *Lucretius,* which owes any beauty it may possess to the proportions of the page, as it has no added ornament except a hand-done initial to each of the six books.

*Lucretius* finished, I started on a companion volume to the folio Dante, *Il Decameron di Boccaccio,* interrupting it to do a small volume for the Poet Laureate, Dr. Robert Bridges. The war put a stop to *Boccaccio* in its early stages, and it was not taken up again until early in 1919. It was issued in 1920. Judging by the price it commands in the market compared with the prices of some of my other books, it doesn't seem to be regarded with much favour by bookbuyers, I do not understand why, as I regard it as a very satisfactory book both from the typographical and literary point of view. A copy of it had the honour a few years ago of being destroyed by the United States postal authorities on the grounds that it was likely to corrupt the morals of their subjects. On complaint being made to them by Messrs Maggs, the forwarders of the copy, the said authorities denied having destroyed the book, but I myself saw the unfortunate copy, or rather its cover, in Messrs Maggs' shop with all the pages cut out to the back margin by a guillotine and a label attached stating that the covers had been returned "as evidence of destruction." I have been fortunate enough to date in escaping prosecution in this country.

After printing two small Italian books in 1921 and 1922, *Vita di S. Chiara* from a fifteenth-century manuscript in my possession and *Fioretti di S. Francesco* with 54 woodcuts by I. Swain from drawings by Charles Gere, I embarked upon another large folio, Spenser's *Faerie Queene*, which occupied the Press for two years, followed at an interval of eighteen months by Spenser's *Minor Poems*.

After using my Subiaco type for more than twenty years I thought that it was about time I had another type cut. I had long admired the type used by Holle of Ulm for the printing of Ptolemy's *Geographia*, and with the assistance of Emery Walker I had this type recut, this time by mechanical means as E. P. Prince was dead and there seemed to be no other available good punch cutter. The result was not unsatisfactory. I decided to use the type for the first time on Shelton's translation of *Don Quixote*, which I printed in two folio volumes between the years 1925 and 1929. Five borders and a large number of initial letters were designed for my use in this book by Louise Powell and cut on wood. They are in my opinion the best initials of their kind that I have seen since those of William Morris, and they are not, like so many initials one sees of kind, merely a base imitation of Morris' work.

My latest book, *Thucydides*, translated by Dr. Jowett, is in folio somewhat smaller than the *Don Quixote*, and printed with long lines instead of in double column. It has side notes in red in another type, the Blado italic of the Monotype Company. This is the first time since my third book issued in 1896 that I have used for side or shoulder notes a type other than that of the book itself.

This *Thucydides* will be the last folio to come from my Press and, I am sorry to add, almost its last book. It will be followed, I hope, by one or two smaller books and by what is commonly called a Catalogue Raisonné of the Press books with specimen pages of many of them. And so will come to a close a Press which has already been in existence thirty years and which has given me an immense amount of pleasure and also of work, but work that was always pleasant and sometimes exciting. I look back without regret of all the time I have spent upon it.

In the choice of books to print I have been influenced partly by my own personal taste in literature and partly by its suitability from the typographical standpoint. That is to say, I have preferred a book which gave some scope for gaiety of treatment by the use of initials and chapter headings in red and blue. There are many books which I should have liked to print had I had the time and the presses — Shakespeare, the English *Bible,* Montaigne's *Essays,* and many others. But it is no use crying over the impossible.

As I said earlier, I have been a Private Press printer entirely for my own pleasure. I do not claim to have done anything original or to have taught printers anything they do not know, or should not have known before. I have followed tradition and, being an admirer of early printing, I have in most of my books followed the tradition of the fifteenth century. I have tried to insist on the use of good materials and the observance of a good rule of proportion in planning my pages and also upon good presswork and accurate register. I should be very proud to think that taken as a whole my books had or will have a good influence upon book production. They may not be to the taste of all typographers and booklovers, but I think I, at least, may say this, that the striving after an ideal, even if that ideal does not meet with general acceptance, is in itself both an incentive and help to those who come after. However much our own work may please us, we should ask for no slavish imitation of it for we know that in printing as in everything else "the letter killeth, but the spirit maketh alive."

-------------

AFTER HORNBY FINISHED his talk, Michael Sadleir, the chairman for the evening, rose and thanked him for his fine presentation of the story of his press. He then called upon several members for comments. Oliver Simon, Francis Meynell, John Johnson, and a man named Wallace, whom I hadn't met but later was told had done Shaw's books, spoke briefly with encomiums. Graily Hewitt rose and said that he was a young barrister when he first met Hornby. I listened with much interest as he talked. I had been studying law when I read the two-volume *Journals* of Cobden-Sanderson, a lawyer who had escaped to a career as a bookbinder and printer. It had converted me from law into hoping to become a printer. I was still not completely certain that my decision had been right. But as Hewitt spoke, looking at Hornby with affection and gratitude, I knew that I had made a happy decision. Hewitt told how Hornby had commissioned him to inscribe the initials and paragraph marks in some of his early books and it had changed his life. He quit law and had a much happier life by devoting it to the crafts.

I had mentioned to Hornby that I had worked on a handpress while in Paris and hoped that on returning to California I could find a handpress on which to print. He thought for a moment and then told me that he hadn't used his original small press for years and he might let me have it. Later he had reservations, and after he closed the press he wrote me that as yet he couldn't bear the thought of parting with anything connected with the press which had been such a joyous part of his life for forty years. I could understand his reluctance.

Ironically, some time after his death in 1946, a large crate arrived at Dawson's Book Shop in Los Angeles from their correspondent bookstore in London, Marks & Co., of 84 Charing Cross Road. When opened it was found to contain hundreds of wood engravings which had been purchased at a country auction in England and sent, without being opened or identified, directly to Dawson's. An astute clerk recognized the engravings as being from the Ashendene Press, and they were snapped up by local collectors as the prices were most modest. My purchases included the engraving of his composing room and two initial letters.

Several years ago I visited Oxford to see the Daniel press, inasmuch as it was identical to my own Albion. Both were made in 1835. While there I was delighted to find also the press Hornby bought in 1900 on which most of his major books had been printed. This led me to wonder what had become of the effects of the Ashendene Press. As I have mentioned, the blocks arrived mysteriously and by chance in Los Angeles and were quickly dispersed. Brooke Crutchley, the distinguished former University printer at Cambridge, wrote me, "We have at the University Press the punches of the Ptolemy and the Subiaco types. No matrices or type exist. Michael Hornby thinks they must have been melted down during the war. Hornby and his mother also gave us a number of sets of sheets of Ashendene volumes, folded and enclosed in boards, but not sewn or bound.

Hornby had them made up so that he could examine them page by page before ordering the binder to go ahead."

In pursuing further the disposition of the Ashendene materials, I heard from Decherd Turner, the director of the Bridwell Library at Southern Methodist University in Dallas, Texas. He wrote, "I purchased the collection of Ashendene books from Michael Hornby, one of the sons of St. John Hornby. Most of our collection is the same as that used for the production of the Ashendene *Bibliography*. Where copies had been printed on vellum, Mr. Hornby's copy was a vellum copy. We already had, or have added since, paper copies to go along with the vellum copies.

"Also present in the Hornby purchase was a collection of letters, ledgers, and a couple of scrapbooks containing some wonderful pieces. The press which Mr. Hornby used from 1900 on to the end of his work is a Hopkinson (no. 2919, built 1853) Albion. This press was indeed at Oxford for some years, but it was there only on loan, not as a gift. So when I made the possession of the press as a prerequisite for the purchase, the Hornby family reclaimed and it is now here.

"As you know the punches of the two founts of type Mr. Hornby used survived; the matrices did not. We have succeeded in getting the matrices rebuilt, and both founts of type are being recast for our usage here.

"One of the most interesting pieces in the collection is a letter from one Ward Ritchie, dated 3 May 1932, in which you say, among other things: 'Now, I am starting a little press of my own, I hope in the same tradition as your great press . . . Really my first production was just finished last week.'"

Hornby died on April 26, 1946, at the age of 78. His close friend, Sir Sydney Cockerell, wrote feelingly of his old companion in the May 10 issue of *The Spectator* entitled modestly "A

Great Printer." In it he mentioned the *Daphnis et Chloe*, which I had watched being set on my visit to Ashendene. It was one of his last beautiful books but as Cockerell recorded, Hornby destroyed all but some ten copies of the original edition when he found that the sheets had been folded before the ink was dry and there was offset on them. He was a perfectionist. Of the books I own, there are few I would consider perfect, especially those printed on a handpress. My mentor in France, François-Louis Schmied, was possibly the most meticulous, printing his many-colored illustrations in exact register with the use of pins. When I look at the Doves books and those of Pissarro at Eragny, I despair of my own trials at handpress printing. But I still use as my guide a book I consider to be impeccable, the Ashendene *Faerie Queene*. My copy may have been specially chosen by Hornby as it was inscribed simply to "Emery Walker from his friend the printer." I haven't found a flaw in register or color. It's perfection in printing.

Cockerell, possibly in premonition of Hornby's imminent death, wrote him in March of 1946, "I had a sudden impulse to treat myself to a feast of Ashendene Press books . . . What a row of typographical masterpieces . . . I felt positively exultant when I went late to bed. I add fresh congratulations and bravos to all of those I sent you in the past."

Hornby replied in a fine summation of his long printing career, "My Press has been the most absorbing interest of my life, and I never tire of thinking over the happy hours I spent in that little room at Shelley House. The satisfaction and pleasure to be got out of a handicraft is known only to those who have experienced it. It is a wonderful relaxation too from all the cares of life and business worries. I wouldn't have been without it for anything."

# 10

## A REQUIEM
### FOR LAWRENCE CLARK POWELL

---

*When Ritchie's boyhood friend, the former librarian and dean of the
Library School at UCLA, approached the age of eighty, Ritchie printed
a small book for the occasion. As so often happens between these
two, it is written in somewhat serious jest.*

---

LAWRENCE CLARK POWELL was born in 1906 in the city of Washington; I had been born the previous year in Los Angeles. Both our families had settled in South Pasadena, then a small suburban town near Los Angeles, by the time we were ready for school. In the subsequent years, we have both been asked on several occasions to memorialize those who have left us. I should regret to have Powell, should I precede him from this life of ours, leave without a few fond words from his oldest friend. Towards this eventuality I have prepared this remembrance. It is what I would wish to say on that occasion.

Powell has written several books recalling his long life of accomplishments which include his autobiography, *Fortune and Friendship,* and its sequel, *Life Goes On.* While they are essentially accurate, I am able to add a few trivial details which he may have overlooked either inadvertently or intentionally.

I have known Powell for over seventy-five years, since grammar school days, and through all of them I have been in awe of his many talents. During our high school years we would often gather at the neighborhood drugstore for a Coca-Cola. Customarily we'd flip Powell's coin to see who was to pay. Powell never did, and that is an early indication of his talent and my gullibility.

As youngsters walking to and from school, we followed meandering paths through the orange groves which then covered most of the area in which we lived. The groves were an integral part of our daily lives. It is quite possible that one of the reasons we are still able to hobble around after all these years is our having been able to pick and eat oranges from the trees whenever we might fancy. And we were also able to build our muscles on the way home from school, often bombarding our friendly enemies with the same fruit. The orange groves were where we could fight wars and play Indians or stealthy games of hide-and-seek among the endless rows of trees.

As I have mentioned many times in introducing him, my first recollection of Powell was on the playground of the Marengo Avenue School, where he dominated us as the "Tyrant of the Teeter-totter."

By the time we had reached the eighth grade, Powell had seemingly shrunk from the physically dominating lad he was in his early years, but he had matured in other ways. A couple of us started a little periodical on which we bestowed the pretentious name of the *Marengo Literary Leader*. Powell's literary reputation was first established in this publication in a piece entitled "The Desert Sunset." Lest it be forever lost in oblivion, I shall here record its opening lines:

> As the sun sank mid billows of golden clouds it cast its last rays of light on the distant purple peaks. A lone night bird, the harbinger of the night, hooted in the distance.

The inspiration for these lines remains a mystery, but his next contribution, "The Purple Dragon," can definitely be attributed to Powell's then fascination with the stories of Sax Rohmer.

We finally graduated into high school. Powell's size eliminated him from participating in football or basketball, and his lack of stamina excluded track. However, with his nimble fingers, he was a sensation on the Typing Team. This pleased him immensely as the other members were girls, in whom he developed a lifelong interest. Aside from his triumphs in typing, he was the fearless cheerleader at all of the athletic events, and the "personification of pep," as the yearbook described him.

College days at Occidental were a pleasant interlude in the life of Powell. The nimble fingers he had conditioned in typing were equally adept on the piano and saxophone with which he entertained his fraternity brothers. He graduated without too much distinction, but he was well-remembered by both faculty and students for several extracurricular escapades.

Two professors of English had a profound influence in shaping our careers. They were Benjamin Stelter, a learned and inspirational man, and Carlyle MacIntyre, an exciting vagabond poet. They so interested us in poetry, literature, and books that we abandoned our previous plans and devoted our lives to books; he as a librarian and author and I as a printer and publisher.

It was not long before both of us were in France pursuing our elusive new careers. He was at the University of Dijon studying for a doctorate in literature, and I was in Paris apprenticed to the great printer and designer François-Louis Schmied. A torrent of letters passed between us, most of which are now preserved in the library at Occidental College. I have kept a few notes from his letters which may give some insight into the views of the youthful Powell.

Any ease of grace or flow of style, or feeling for words, which my writing may possess, has been long and slow in coming — and at this very epoch, I find it desperately hard to write anything decent; every sentence and word demand concentration. But it gets easier as time goes by — and eventually I hope to have trained my subconscious that I can sweep along at good speed.

---

I have a small frame and a Big spirit. Is there more to say?

---

Whenever I think of the problem of Form and Feeling, I go straight to Bach and Mozart. There the strictest possible forms are molds for a tremendous range of feeling. God, what a glorious combination is there.

---

Let destiny sweep us down with its peristaltic motion.

---

Keep marching — we're on the road to renown if not riches.

And this was written on the graveside of D.H. Lawrence in Vence, where he was first buried:

God, Richman, I sit here in the hot lazy afternoon sun on the small sweet grass and I see the little flowering Phoenix-crowned grave, a shiny black bumblebee exploring the anemones, the gnats dancing in the western light; and hear the distant dogs barking, cocks crowing — and I wonder what strange affinity brought me clear across the world to sit here and muse and write a note to you. And I wonder where on this earth you and I are to sleep finally. Everywhere there are graves — the living and the dead — who are the more potent? . . . No man could wish for a more lovely last resting place than Lawrence's. I shall carry the sweet memory of my little pilgrimage down to my own end. I lay there on the grass and prayed that I be worthy, generous and kind and tender and faithful — may we all be.

With his doctorate from the University of Dijon, Powell returned home to California during the worst of the Depression. Without a job he married his college sweetheart, Fay Ellen Shoemaker. To keep them from starving, Jake Zeitlin gave

Larry work in his bookshop. Eventually he was able to spend a year at the University of California at Berkeley adding another degree in library science. Soon he was working at the library at the University of California at Los Angeles as an acquisitions clerk. That was in 1938, and for the next twenty-eight years he devoted most of his time to that institution, as director of the Clark Library, university librarian, and dean of the Library School. At the time of his original employment, the library had fewer than 300,000 volumes. I well remember that fact since the acquisition of the 300,000th volume was celebrated with much fanfare. Through Powell's wily machinations, my publication of *Robinson Jeffers* by William van Wyck just happened to be the book chosen for that honor. During his administration, 2 million more volumes were subsequently added to make the University of California at Los Angeles library one of the foremost research libraries of the nation.

In 1966 he retired at the age of sixty, hoping to devote his remaining years to writing. However, he was soon persuaded to become professor in residence at the University of Arizona. Fortunately he was allowed plenty of free time to explore the Southwest. Books and articles poured from his typewriter, and he became the esteemed chronicler of the Southwest, just as he had been of California before his defection.

I have known the "Goose," as I affectionately refer to him, for a full lifetime, more years than many are privileged to live. I enjoy numerous good memories of him. I wish I could fill in all of the nooks and crannies of this man's life, but he has done a fairly respectable job of that for himself, as I have previously mentioned. He generously described our relationship in his autobiography, *Fortune and Friendship:* "We were unlike in every way. Ritchie was relaxed, I was compulsive; he quiet, I noisy; he gentle, I rough. He was tall, thin, blond; I was short, chunky, dark. But we clicked, in the attraction of opposites. Throughout the years we have never had the faintest misunderstandings, the credit being his, not mine."

Fortune favored me also, not only for allowing me to survive these many score years, but also to enjoy them with the likes of Lawrence Clark Powell.

# 11

## VIRGINIA CITY
### AND THE GENESIS OF A COOKBOOK

*During the 1950s the flamboyant Lucius Beebe and a couple of
female journalists descended upon the ghost town of Virginia City,
Nevada, and managed for a few years to rekindle the robust liveliness of
the town's early glory days. It is a cookbook, oddly enough, that has best
chronicled the festive gaiety they nourished.*

THE KATIES WERE A LIVELY, fun-loving pair, writing in tandem.
They burst unexpectedly into our lives early in the 1950s,
searching for a story they could peddle to *McCall's* magazine,
which willingly published most of their collaborations. They
continually bounced around the country gathering material and
ideas for articles or books they might write. Somewhere they
had run across a copy of one of the cookbooks by Helen Evans
Brown we had published. Helen Brown's recipes were original
and elegant, and the pages were made more interesting for the
casual reader by the addition of apt and curious quotations
about cooking gathered by her husband Philip. Once the Katies
had communicated with the Browns we became involved, and
there began a relationship lasting for many years that fostered a
cookbook.

The Katies were both worldly-wise and quite rowdy in an
amusing way. Katie Best was the more soft-spoken, a bit pudgy

and sweet-tempered. Katie Hillyer was a striking blonde with classic features, a truly beautiful woman, but hardly a lady. Best was a Southerner, from Kentucky, while Hillyer was a true Westerner whose grandparents had been among the boisterous residents of Virginia City, Nevada, during the 1870s. It was a wild town then, known as "The Queen of the Comstock," with silver wealth pouring out of the mines creating a mixture of opulent culture and frontier rowdyism — Piper's Opera House competing with a hundred saloons for the locals' attention.

The Hillyer house in Virginia City, where the Katies headquartered, was slightly down the hillside from the center of Virginia City activity, but unfortunately within too easy walking distance, which eventually contributed to the Katies' undoing. They had restored the house in quaint Victorian elegance with a four-poster bed, a hand-painted, four-legged bathtub, and gas lamps. The flamboyant Lucius Beebe and his companion, Charles Clegg, had recently moved there, buying an old mansion as well as the long defunct newspaper, *The Territorial Enterprise.* Beebe envisioned, through the paper, restoring to the town some of the glamour and gusto of its bygone days when Mark Twain and Dan de Quille created their own version of news for the paper. While their antics amused many, they irritated others. It is reported that the editor on one occasion observed one of the habitual patrons of the Sazarac Bar perusing a copy of the town's other paper. Rather annoyed, he asked the fellow, "How come?" The caustic reply was, "I read this paper for the news and I use the *Enterprise* to wipe my bottom." "Keep that up," was the immediate retort, "and your bottom will be smarter than you."

Beebe was a socialite, an epicure, a boulevardier, "Mr. New York," and a columnist for the *New York Herald Tribune* before making his move west to Virginia City in 1950. He always enjoyed being the center of attention and always acted the part of the elegant *bon vivant*. Even as a young man while attending Harvard College he began creating this image of himself. While dining lavishly at an elegant restaurant he would often hire a street urchin to weather the cold of the night and press his nose against the windowpane from the outside and watch hungrily as Beebe leisurely enjoyed his meal. In reviving *The Territorial Enterprise* and moving to Virginia City, Beebe nostalgically hoped to recreate in miniature his version of the opulence and turbulence of the late nineteenth century with his contemporaries watching from the outside in envy.

Under Beebe's guidance *The Enterprise* managed to recapture much of this liveliness and gusto, in part due to his being able to persuade the Katies to spend more time in Virginia City and contribute to the paper a weekly column called "Comstock Vignettes." It absorbed more and more of their time as they wandered through The Bucket of Blood, The Brass Rail, The Delta, The Sazarac, and a half-dozen more of the local bars gathering interesting tidbits of gossip they could transform into amusing material for their column. In the early days it was the accepted custom that any patron of a bar was entitled to an early morning "stiffener," free of charge, to help him face the advent of another day. It is said that some customers took advantage of this quaint custom and visited several of the bars for their free sample before seriously indulging. While this practice was no longer observed, the Katies managed to collect enough free drinks on their rounds to make the days quite enjoyable. However, it was not too financially rewarding, and the ever-present gaming tables managed to siphon off any lingering cash they might have. Katie Hillyer, especially, was a compulsive gambler. Realizing their plight, the Browns suggested collaborating on a cookbook combining both the past and present Virginia City.

The Katies were delighted with the idea and immediately

began soliciting the patrons of the various saloons they patronized to produce their favorite recipes. The Browns researched historic recipes and gathered bits of early lore about Virginia City. We induced Harry Diamond to illustrate the book and Lucius Beebe to write an introduction. Beebe recalled the days when Virginia City was San Francisco's most sumptuous suburb and frequently even eclipsed its famed neighbor in culinary extravagance. He mentioned that "Comstockers began to accustom themselves to champagne in double magnums and the proprieties of highlife generally. A particularly durable English lord was guest of honor at a dinner at the International Hotel where 6,000 bottles of champagne were opened. Everybody, to be sure, really preferred whiskey, but sparkling wine was the currency of elegance and therefore *de rigueur*. Much of the community was in a state of *rigueur* as a consequence."

From the Katies' interviews and questioning of more than a hundred of the town's more interesting characters, they were able to compile along with the Browns *The Virginia City Cook Book*. They wrote with wit and charm, often with tongue in cheek, as the following samples of a few of the recipes will attest.

### FOUR-DAY JACK'S FIVE-WAY MULLIGAN

The Delta Cafe's *chef de cuisine* is famous for his Hungarian goulash, his Irish stew, his braised sirloin tips, his jungle mulligan, and his beef ragout. That they all come from the same pot makes no difference to his patrons. What they like is variety, and at the Delta they get it:

Braise lean beef in olive oil, or olive oil and lard. Add sliced onions and minced garlic, and brown with the meat which is stirred constantly. Now add, to taste, peperino (that's thyme), rosemary, paprika, salt and pepper. When nicely browned, add canned tomatoes — not too many and stir a bit until the brew is thick. Season with salt and pepper, add some flour and soup stock, and simmer with vegetables. The amounts? It depends on how many regulars are in town and on the tourist expectancy. Four-Day Jack didn't say so, but we think this pot, thinned with stock, is his vegetable soup; topped with crust, his meat pie; mingled with beans, his chili and beans; and doused with sour cream, his beef stroganoff!

### SAZARAC CHILI AND BEANS

It never occurred to Ole Hart and Clint Andreasen, proprietors of the Sazarac Saloon, that their chili would compete in customer popularity with the huge painting of the murder of famed Madame Julie Bulette which hangs over their bar, or the old Agency Bank vault in the back. But it does. That means it's quite a chili.

Soak 2 pounds of pinto beans overnight, then cook with 2 ham hocks until tender. Make a sauce with 1½ pounds of ground beef, 2 large or 3 small onions, chopped, 1 clove of garlic, pressed, and a chopped green pepper — this all cooked until wilted in ¼ cup of olive oil. Then 3 cans of tomato paste are added, also salt and pepper, and about a quart of water, as well as plenty of chili powder (about a third of a can). This is all simmered for 2 hours, or cooked in a pressure cooker for 30 minutes, then combined with the undrained beans. The meat from the ham hocks is pulled from the bones and added too.

### SILVER DOLLAR CORN FRITTERS

Florence Ballou Edwards told us about these tasty little fritters and we have named them in honor of her Silver Dollar Hotel. Florence, a former Bostonian, became proprietress of the Silver Dollar back in 1946 and instituted several managerial customs not ordinarily associated with the hostelry trade. For instance, she runs the place with signs — there's one saying "Ring Cowbell for Clerk" (there is no clerk) and another saying "Call Upstairs for Manager" (the manager is usually elsewhere). Her rooms are named for famous old bonanza-day characters, like Hank Monk and Lola Montez and Mark Twain, and guests carry their own bags. Mrs. Edwards especially likes guests who can cook and when we interviewed her she was saying goodbye to a guest of Greek extraction and greeting one of Austrian. "Last month," she said, "I lived on thyme, parsley, and honey. This month I expect to live on paprika, caraway, and nutmeg. Next month it will probably be chili, cumin, and oregano — my spice cabinet is getting low."

Score 4 ears of golden bantam corn by running a sharp knife down the center of each row of kernels. Scrape corn into a bowl, being sure to salvage all the juices. Separate 2 eggs, beat the yolks until light, add the corn and ½ teaspoon of salt, then fold in the egg whites which have been beaten until stiff. Drop from a teaspoon into plenty of butter in a skillet. They should be no larger than a silver dollar. Fry on both sides until brown, and serve them at once, and don't be surprised if even the dainty feeders stow away a dozen or more. (With bacon and fried or broiled tomatoes, maybe?)

### MRS. MC BRIDE'S GALLINA WITH POLENTA

The V.L. McBrides came to Virginia City about twenty years ago and opened their noted saloon-museum, The Bucket of Blood, an establishment crammed with fascinating bonanza-day loot — a million pieces in all, it's said. Mac wears in his vest the great gold watch presented by George Hearst and Horace Greeley to Hank Monk, the famous stagecoach driver, on which are engraved Hank's immortal words, "Keep your seat, Mr. Greeley, I'll get you there." When Mrs. Mac is cooking one of her delectable dishes upstairs over the saloon, the customers downstairs start sniffing like crazy, especially if it's her gallina.

Have a large colored hen disjointed and cut in serving pieces, and brown it in olive oil. When very well colored pour off all but 1 tablespoonful of the fat in the pan. Mash a small clove of garlic (smash it with a cleaver, says Mrs. McB.) and cook it in the fat along with a couple of leaves of fresh (preferably) sage and a sprig of fresh thyme. Now add 2 tablespoons of tomato sauce or $^1/_2$ tablespoon of tomato paste dissolved in a couple of tablespoons of water. Cook 5 minutes. Put chicken back in large skillet and simmer until tender, adding water as necessary, a cup at a time. When the chicken is tender, add a pound of mushroom caps and a large can of pitted ripe olives. The gravy should be a medium brown — thicken it, but not much. Serve with polenta.

### CHARLES ADDIS' MIDNIGHT OYSTER STEW

Charlie Addis, when sufficiently prodded and lubricated, confessed that he did, indeed, cook himself a meal after leaving the brights lights of C Street. Charlie is seen on the boulevard from very early eye-opener to very late nightcap, so we can but assume that his repast is a post-midnight one. It consists of "something from a can," a favorite being oyster stew.

Heat a can of milk and a can of oysters together, add a big lump of butter and some salt and pepper, and $^1/_2$ cup of white wine or sherry. That's Charlie's way. When using fresh oysters, use a pint of them to a pint of half-and-half and a pint of milk. Heat the milk and cream, add a big piece of butter (2 tablespoons) and the oysters. Season with salt and pepper and allow to stand for a few hours. When time to serve, add a little sherry or white wine, if you wish, heat to just under the boil, and serve with parsley or paprika sprinkled on the top. Pilot biscuits are good with this.

The Katies seldom wasted time cooking for themselves. In fact Katie Hillyer commented that she had never had the time nor the inclination to learn. But since they were presumably the authors of the book, Helen Brown created a few recipes to be included under their names. Their contribution, in addition to the footwork in collecting much of the material included, was a sparkling introduction dubbed "Virginia City, Liveliest Ghost Town in the World." It is well worth quoting.

———————

Today you can see almost all that's left of Virginia City, Nevada, by pivoting on one heel in front of the Bucket of Blood Saloon — all that's left of a fantastically wealthy and sophisticated metropolis of the 1860s and 1870s when 45,000 people lived here and the billion-dollar Comstock Lode was being torn out in hunks and nuggets and drayloads of gold and silver. The town in those days was a phenomenon of civilization on the American frontier, for Virginia City wasn't built by austere pioneers. It was built, suddenly, by mansion-minded men, an amalgamation of the few who struck it rich by pickaxe and the many who came as scientists, engineers, editors, lawyers, bankers, and businessmen to make a fast buck with their brains.

These men had preconceived notions of good living which they quickly sought to satisfy by importing items like Italian marble and tapestries for their elaborate Victorian homes, oysters and *pâté de foie gras* and champagne for their tables, actors such as Edwin Booth and Maude Adams and Modjeska for their amusement, palms and plush for their restaurants and clubs. Everybody who was anybody in those days, from Tom Thumb to President Grant, came out to see this fabulous cosmopolis known as "the most important city between Chicago and the Pacific Ocean."

And all were overwhelmed by Virginia City's opulent way of

life — its six first-class hotels, the most noted of which was the spectacular International, boasting the first elevator west of Chicago; its twenty theaters and music halls of which Piper's Opera House was the most famous, where audiences in evening dress and diamonds arrived in fine carriages drawn by horses harnessed with silver bullion; its clubs and restaurants, where chefs of international reputation produced repasts of sumptuous splendor; its famous Virginia and Truckee Railroad, which wound up and over the mountains twice daily, often bringing some titan of finance or a foreign notable in his private palace car.

Yes, Virginia was quite a city in those days. Its mighty riches transformed a piddling port town on the Pacific into San Francisco; they jacked up to victory the precariously financed Northern armies during the Civil War; they put telegraph lines across the continent and cables under the oceans. They financed the Central Pacific Railroad and the Wells Fargo Company. They produced millionaires by the score.

But everything was not champagne and *pâté de foie gras* and unmitigated splendor. In the course of her hectic, history-heavy career, Virginia City fought off an attack by the Piute Indians, survived a snowbound winter of near-starvation, time and again rebuilt itself after windstorms and fires crisscrossed the mountainsides with paths of destruction. One holocaust, the "Great Fire" of 1875, destroyed property valued at $10,000,000 and laid nine-tenths of the celebrated city in ruins. A little later, when barren borasco succeeded bonanza and the town emptied like a jug turned upside down, the tenacious handful of people who remained began what might be called Virginia City's cold war with ghosthood.

Since then there have been mild booms and sinking spells but the Great Bonanza was gone for good. Today there are fewer than 500 people living in Virginia City and all the great mines and mills are shut down. Only here and there can you see physical signs of the town's former architectural opulence. Piper's Opera House, Graves Castle, St. Mary's in the Mountains, the Fourth Ward School, the Court House, the old Nevada Brewery — these are a few fine old structures which have survived time and the elements. An occasional gaunt mansion and the trembly ruin of a once-notable building spot the hills in blitz-like melancholy. The crumbly plank sidewalks of C Street, where once trod the great of a distinguished era, now billow beneath the feet of that ubiquitous, peripatetic American known as the tourist.

But what is left is like a slug of raw history. The town pulsates with virile traditions and its people regard the florid past with a sentimental and history-wary eye. There is a vivid, easy-come, easy-go personality that makes Virginia City unique among the small towns of America. And nowhere else in all this land of plenty will you find a more sophisticated and uninhibited love of good food. Virginia City, to be perfectly arbitrary about it, is a town of gourmets.

There are probably as many reasons why Virginia Citians eat well as there are Virginia Citians, but the primary explanations seem to be that there is a hallowed gustatory reputation to uphold and a present-day population of almost as many nationalities as the United Nations. Yank and Rebel, Italian, Basque, Polish, French, German, Spanish, Dutch, Irish, English, Welsh, Chinese, Czech, Greek, Scot, Jew, Finn, Yugoslav, Indian and one roguish Martinique. Virginia City couldn't produce an uninteresting meal if it wanted to, and we don't think there's any better way to tell the story of our town than to tell about its flamboyant and remarkable cosmopolitan eating customs.

Publication of *The Virginia City Cook Book* was an event of carnival importance to the town. Almost every inhabitant could be seen wandering from bar to bar proudly flaunting his or her contribution and trading autographs. That was over thirty-five years ago, and few of those involved are now among the living. Helen Brown died in 1964 and the Katies followed soon after. Katie Best, gradually going blind, returned to Kentucky to die with her family. Katie Hillyer, left alone in Virginia City, slowly drank herself to death. Beebe and Clegg abandoned the town and left their once-lively *Enterprise* to die once again.

Virginia City can hardly be the same nowadays without Beebe's flamboyant life style enlivening the town, without the Katies rollicking through the bars, and without the rambunctious *Enterprise* creating a model of behaviour for the townsfolk to emulate. I wistfully remember our many visits to this crumbling town those many years ago and wonder if any of the vigor of those few boisterous years of its temporary revival still lingers on.

# INDEX

---

Five hundred copies, designed by Ward Ritchie, were printed by the Premier Printing Corporation for Dawson's Book Shop. The author offers thanks for editorial suggestions to Gloria Stuart, Fay and Lawrence Clark Powell, Glen and Muir Dawson, Dana C. Cordrey, and Martha Fares.